An Introduction to Teaching Composition in an Electronic Environment

An Introduction to Teaching Composition in an Electronic Environment

Eric Hoffman
Northern Illinois University

Carol Scheidenhelm
Northern Illinois University

Allyn and Bacon
Boston   London   Toronto   Sydney   Tokyo   Singapore

Copyright © 2000 by Allyn & Bacon
A Pearson Education Company
160 Gould Street
Needham Heights, Massachusetts 02494-2130

Internet: www.abacon.com

All rights reserved. No part of the material protected by this copyright notice
may be reproduced or utilized in any form or by any means, electronic or
mechanical, including photocopying, recording, or by any information
storage and retrieval system, without the written permission of the copyright owner.

ISBN 0-205-29715-3

Printed in the United States of America

10 9 8 7 6 5 4 3 2 1   03 02 01 00

Preface

At Northern Illinois University (NIU), the English Department requires that every section of freshman English (roughly 130 sections per semester) meets at least once a week in a computer lab. I am directly responsible for training those teachers how to teach in an electronic environment, and Carol, who works in the Faculty Development and Instructional Design Center, has a similar role campus wide. The teachers I train are mostly graduate students and part-time instructors; they typically are people who do not have new computers at home, nor money to purchase them, and who do not have extra time to devote to learning technological applications of pedagogy on their own. On the whole, these teachers are average computer users; they can word-process, use e-mail, and browse the Web, but they have never explored the various functions of any of these programs. Most importantly, they have had neither training nor experience related to using these tools in a composition classroom. They are excellent teachers, however, and are willing to learn so long as they can see how these new tools can be used to enhance their classes.

To supplement our training program, Carol and I began to search for a textbook that might help our teachers learn the basics of technology integration. To our dismay, we found very few textbooks concerning technology that were written for teachers of composition at a college level, and of the few we found, most operated at a level of composition theory that our teachers didn't find helpful. Our teachers wanted practical explanations and specific ideas for lesson plans that they could incorporate into their classes.

This book is designed to provide that introduction. We avoid a discussion of Computer Mediated Composition (CMC) theory, because such discussions tend to be expressed in exclusionary academic jargon, and because our audience needs a practical introduction to using these tools. For the same reason that we don't teach advanced composition theory to our freshman in core curriculum writing courses, we don't flood teachers new to technology with advanced CMC theory. We do recommend that our teachers enter these academic and professional dialogues once they have become familiar with the basics of teaching in an electronic environment, by attending professional conferences or joining such mailing lists as the Alliance for Computers and Writing (information available at <http://english.ttu.edu/acw/>), or the World Web Wide in Education list (subscription information at <http://edweb.gsn.org/wwwedu.html>).

This book is divided into two main sections. The first section explains the basics of the three main computer tools used in composition courses (word processor, e-mail, and the World Wide Web), and discusses some of the basic ways in which these tools can be implemented in the classroom. This section assumes some basic knowledge on the part of the user, but we have tried to explain the major concepts and terminology used in relation to these tools.

The second section of the book addresses more directly the application of technology in the classroom. It includes practical advice about preparing for a course with an electronic component, and what to do on the first few days in the lab. This section also includes a series of lesson plans categorized according to pedagogical goals and technological requirements. These lesson plans are activities that have been used in class here at NIU, and we have suggested ways in which the lessons could be modified or adapted for teachers who want to personalize the activities.

These two sections should play off each other. The first section provides the background knowledge necessary to implement the lesson plans in the second section. The second section provides activities that teachers can easily adapt for their own classes, and helps teachers create their own lessons by providing specific examples of the kinds of techniques presented in the first section.

A third supplementary section of this text includes a number of resources our teachers have requested, including trouble-shooting guides for common problems in the lab, a glossary of computer terms, sample Web pages that teachers can adapt for their courses, a section on Netiquette, and an index of on-line writing and grammar resources on the Web.

Our goal has been to present these concepts in a friendly and accessible manner. Technology can offer some wonderful opportunities for composition courses, but we understand how easy it is to feel intimidated by computers and cyber-culture. We hope this text helps make technology more accessible, and ultimately, that it helps teachers do their jobs effectively.

Eric Hoffman

April 22, 1999

Table of Contents

PREFACE 1

TABLE OF CONTENTS 4

CHAPTER 1: TEACHING WRITING IN AN ELECTRONIC ENVIRONMENT 8
- IMPLICATIONS OF USING TECHNOLOGY IN THE CLASSROOM 8
- WHY TEACH WITH TECHNOLOGY? 11
- TEACHING WITH TECHNOLOGY, NOT TEACHING TECHNOLOGY 12
- WHAT TO EXPECT FROM THIS TEXT 14
- CONVENTIONS 15
- WORDS OF ENCOURAGEMENT 15
- WORKS CITED 16

CHAPTER 2: SOME GUIDING PRINCIPLES 17
- INTEGRATION 17
- SIMPLICITY 20
- CONSISTENCY 22
- PREPARATION 23
- IMPROVISATION 25
- (TROUBLESHOOTING EXPERIENCE) 27

CHAPTER 3: WORD-PROCESSING BASICS 29
- WORD PROCESSOR TYPES 29
- THE FULL-FEATURED WORD PROCESSOR 30
  - Advantages of the Full-Featured Word Processor 30
  - Disadvantages of the Full-Featured Word Processor 31
- THE BARE-BONES WORD PROCESSOR 32
  - Disadvantages of the Bare-Bones Word Processor 32
  - Advantages of the Bare-Bones Word Processor 33
- CHOOSING A WORD PROCESSOR 34
- WORD-PROCESSING STANDARDIZATION 35
- SAVING 36
- ENSURE FILE TRANSLATABILITY THROUGH REDUNDANT FILE SAVES 39
- CUT, COPY, AND PASTE 39
- FIND/REPLACE 41
- SPELL CHECK/ GRAMMAR CHECK 42
- USING HELP 43

CHAPTER 4: USING THE WORD PROCESSOR IN CLASS 44
- THE WORD PROCESSOR AS WRITING SPACE 45
- THE WORD PROCESSOR AS REVISION TOOLBOX 46
- THE WORD PROCESSOR AS A MEDIUM OF COLLABORATION 48
- THE WORD PROCESSOR AS A DESKTOP PUBLISHER 50
- WORD-PROCESSING IN A LOCAL AREA NETWORK 53

CHAPTER 5: E-MAIL BASICS 59
GETTING AN ACCOUNT 59
PASSWORD TIPS 60
CHOOSING A MAIL READER 61
THE CLIENT-SIDE MAIL READER 61
SERVER-SIDE E-MAIL APPLICATIONS 65
Telnet 65
Web-Based E-mail Programs 66
USING MAIL FOLDERS 68
NEWSGROUPS AND MAILING LISTS 68
Newsgroups 69
Mailing Lists 69

CHAPTER 6: USING E-MAIL IN CLASS 71
GUIDELINES SPECIFYING ACCEPTABLE AND EXPECTED USE 72
E-MAIL AS A WRITING SPACE 73
ASYNCHRONOUS SPACE OF PUBLIC DISCOURSE 74
E-mail as Classroom Supplement 75
"Flame-Retardant" Discourse 77
E-mail as Publication 79
Critical "Lurking" 81
E-MAIL ATTACHMENTS 83
Attachments and Viruses 84

CHAPTER 7: WORLD WIDE WEB BASICS 86
HOW WEB PAGES WORK 87
HTML 89
Graphics 89
Interactive Elements 91
"Java" and Advanced Scripting Languages 92
Other Protocols 92
USING A WEB BROWSER 93
Other Options 98
UNDERSTANDING URL'S 99
Protocol 99
Server Name and Domain 100
File Path 101
File Name 102
SELECT RESOURCES RELATED TO WEB PAGES 103

CHAPTER 8: SEARCH ENGINES 104
HOW SEARCH ENGINES WORK 104
CHOOSING A SEARCH ENGINE 106
Refining a Search 107
SEARCH TECHNIQUES 108
Domain-Name Search 108
Specific Content Search 109
Context Search 110
EVALUATING SEARCH RESULTS 112
Page Content and Design 112
URL Evaluation 114
Backtracking 115
Attribution and Contacts 116
Outside References or Citations 117
SELECTED SEARCH ENGINE AND INTERNET EVALUATION RESOURCES 119

CHAPTER 9: INTEGRATING WEB INSTRUCTION 121
  TYPES OF INTEGRATION 121
  WEB-SUPPORTED INSTRUCTION 122
    Course Syllabus 124
    Creating an On-Line Course Syllabus 126
    Reading Materials and Resource Links 127
    Virtual Discussion Groups 128
  WEB-BASED INSTRUCTION 130
    Daily Assignments 130
  CHAT ROOMS 134
    MOO's, MUD's 136
  SELECT RESOURCES RELATED TO TEACHING AND THE WORLD WIDE WEB 138

CHAPTER 10: PREPARING THE ELECTRONIC ENVIRONMENT 139
  DEFINE GOALS 140
  IDENTIFY RESOURCES 140
    Hardware 141
    Hardware Checklist 142
    Software 142
    Software Checklist 144
    Support 147
    Technical Support Checklist 147
  MATCH GOALS WITH RESOURCES 148

CHAPTER 11: ENTERING THE ELECTRONIC ENVIRONMENT 151
  BEFORE GOING TO LAB 151
  DAY ONE 153
  SUGGESTIONS FOR FIRST DAY ACTIVITIES 155
    Interactive/Continuous Narrative ("musical computers") 155
    First-Day Reaction Statement 156
  DAY TWO 157
  SUGGESTIONS FOR SECOND DAY ACTIVITIES 158
    Comparative Summaries 158
    Second Day Reaction Statement 159

CHAPTER 12: WORD-PROCESSING LESSON PLAN SAMPLES 160
  Collaborative Word-Processing Stories 162
  Freewriting Journal 163
  Spellcheck: Text Manipulation Activity 164
  Select, Cut, Copy and Paste 166
  Works Cited Information Collection 168
  Spellcheck Journal 170
  Charting Personal Writing Problems 172
  Peer Interviews for a Case Study 173
  Problem Solving: Investigating and Recommending Specific Action 175
  Rewriting Exercise 178

CHAPTER 13: LESSON PLANS USING E-MAIL 179
  Diagnostic Exercise 182
  E-mail Discussion 184
  Introductions 186
  Holiday Season Rituals 187
  Small Group Brainstorming and Topic Selection 189
  Writing for Different Audiences 190
  Individual/ Small Group "Oral" Reports 192
  Critical "Lurking" 193

CHAPTER 14: WEB-BASED LESSON PLANS 195
- Diagnostic Exercise (version 1) 197
- Diagnostic Exercise (version 2) 198
- Final Exam 199
- Citation Style Treasure Hunt 201
- Search Engine Topic Exploration 202
- Web Page Credibility 204
- Hypertext Reading 206

APPENDIX A: GLOSSARY 208

APPENDIX B: WRITING BASIC COURSE WEB PAGES 216
- USING THE TEMPLATE 216
- GENERAL HTML INSTRUCTIONS 217
- WEB PAGE TEMPLATE 219
  - Blank Template 220
  - HTML Script for the Blank Template 221
  - Partially Filled-out Web script 224
  - Completed Web Page 226
- HTML SOURCES FOR LESSON PLANS INCLUDED IN CHAPTER 14 228
  - Diagnostic Exercise (version 1) 228
  - Diagnostic Exercise (version 2) 229
  - Final Exam 230

APPENDIX C: NETIQUETTE, EMOTICONS AND ACRONYMS 233
- NETIQUETTE 233
- EMOTICONS AND ACRONYMS 235

APPENDIX D: TROUBLESHOOTING GUIDES 237
- BASIC WORD-PROCESSING TROUBLESHOOTING 237
  - Opening Files 238
  - Saving and Printing Files 239
- E-MAIL TROUBLESHOOTING 240
  - Sending 240
  - Receiving 242
- WORLD WIDE WEB TROUBLESHOOTING 244
  - File Not Found 244
  - File Type Unknown 246

APPENDIX E: ON-LINE WRITING AND GRAMMAR RESOURCES 250

APPENDIX F: SELECT BIBLIOGRAPHY 252

Chapter 1

Teaching Writing in an Electronic Environment

As teachers of composition, we are called upon to have an enormous collage of skills, all of which must be honed to a level that requires superior proficiency. In our repertoire of competencies, we must determine an approach for creatively teaching focus, organization, substance, and meaning to a group of often reluctant students who believe they have heard it all before. So when we are asked -- or required -- to add yet another measurable behavior to the already hefty list of curricular objectives, even the most dedicated among us might sigh, wondering how to fit anything else into a tightly packed syllabus. What is different about integrating a technology component, however, is that unlike an additional assignment highlighting a particular writing mode, adding technology can heighten *all* aspects of what is already in place. Technology becomes a valuable means by which to enliven and contemporize the writing curriculum.

Implications of Using Technology in the Classroom

While most of what we will be discussing in this text involves the use of computers in instruction, we will generally use the more universal terms technology, instructional/educational technologies, and computer-mediated composition (CMC) to describe the computer component of a course. These terms are good descriptors, for though the reality of technology use in the typical writing course centers on computers, the scope of what those computers facilitate when used for e-mail, the Internet, and other instructive media seems diminished when referred to simply as "computer use."

Perhaps the most formidable task involved when integrating technology into the writing curriculum is maintaining both the vitality and integrity of the course. In our zeal, we tend to focus on the aspects of technology that emphasize economy of time and energy. Alan Kay, one of the founders of Xerox Palo Alto Research, warns "technology often forces us to choose between quality and convenience" (152). The danger in this choice, Kay warns, is that when "convenience is valued over quality in education, we are led to 'junk' learning" (153). Many who oppose the use of instructional technologies in the writing classroom echo Kay's concern. More often than not, experienced faculty who oppose the use of technology are genuinely concerned that the electronic media may lead to irrelevant or unproductive learning; they realize that introducing this new component will drastically alter the successful patterns they have worked to establish. As a colleague and veteran teacher of writing would repeatedly ask: "how does technology make my students better writers?" She was not opposed to learning about teaching in a networked environment but was concerned that the vast amounts of time required to incorporate this skill would detract from her focus on writing. This text hopes to expand the question of technology's effectiveness as a means to make students better writers; the enhanced query becomes "what pedagogical impact does technology have on the learning process?"

Most would agree that technology does not make us better teachers; good teaching is good teaching with or without technology (just as bad teaching is not improved by technology). As educational technology coordinator Michelle Lamberson contends, "Educational malpractice [ineffectual teaching] . . . can happen regardless of the delivery method. Anyone can give just as poor a lecture with PowerPoint as with chalk" (Bollentin 52). We have all witnessed the wretched excess of technology as well as the simple effectiveness of traditional teaching excellence.

Whether the integration of CMC will have a positive or negative impact on improving instruction cannot be predicted. But most critics agree that restructuring a curriculum for *any* reason forces the instructor to examine and re-evaluate course goals. As we investigate the many ways the Internet can enliven a particular course assignment, for example, we might determine that the activity is passé. The new technology may provide a more timely activity to fulfill the writing objective.

There are, and will continue to be, many detractors. This book is an attempt to directly answer those who are motivated enough to ask how technology will make students better writers. It is our intent to outline a method whereby instructors are encouraged to use technology as integral to the writing process, not a separate skill but an improved method for teaching skills already targeted in the writing curriculum. We have based the book on the following premises:

(1) The primary objective of every lesson is the writing objective.

(2) The teacher is a *writing* expert, not a technology expert.

(3) Technology should not be used as an end in itself but should be embedded into the course.

(4) Students will use technology if they have a compelling reason to do so. Put another way, if the instructor sees no value in instructional technology, neither will the student.

One aspect of education will not be changed by education technologies: students will continue to look to the instructor for direction. Technology increases quantities of information; it takes a "director" to assist students in processing that information so that it becomes knowledge. Through the outline of objectives and activities provided in this text, the instructor can orchestrate the acquisition and processing of information while maintaining integrity in the writing process.

Why Teach with Technology?

If there are no guarantees that using technology will improve instruction, why take the chance of creating nothing more than "junk learning"? Education is about taking chances -- calculated chances designed to motivate and intrigue students. The electronic medium is not going away; instead, the world is being redefined in terms of rapid transfer of information and virtual communication. Composition studies must also evolve as society and the corporate world expand the scope of what role writing will play. CMC can prepare students for the collaborative writing projects they will participate in as they venture into the business world, while still providing a solid base of traditional writing proficiency. Knowledge of scholarly use of the Internet and e-mail assists students in understanding the challenges and advantages of timely information and the immediacy of harnessing that information.

Educational analyst Monty Neill provides the following reasons why use of computers in education has value: (1) Educational tools enable students to spend time on reasoning and problem-solving rather than mechanics. (2) Since many schools cannot continuously update library and other on-site resources, the computer network provides enhanced access to current information. (3) The Internet provides connectivity to an expanded pool of people who can be used as resources. (4) Students can work on more sophisticated and realistic problems using computerized tools (419). Our challenge as educators is to use the strengths of information technologies to provide students with a challenging forum in which to develop skills appropriate for the demands of contemporary productivity.

Teaching With Technology, NOT Teaching Technology

One of the more often-voiced concerns of faculty teaching with technology has revolved around the philosophy that it becomes the instructor's job to teach computer use to students. It would be foolhardy to deny this claim any legitimacy; we *do* become responsible for helping students figure out the *how*. By acknowledging that students will need extra instruction using the classroom tools, instructors can minimize their direct involvement in the actual process of teaching students how to use technology.

Perhaps the most beneficial strategy for dealing with technical instruction is the advanced planning that follows in the wake of such acknowledgement. Such foresight encourages the shift of responsibility for perfecting technical skills from faculty to student. Listed are a few suggestions for nudging your students into the self-learning mode:

- Administer a simple diagnostic to determine their level of computer competency.
- Check to see if the campus computing agency offers introductory courses for students. Require students who perform poorly on the diagnostic to attend. If no such workshops exist, request them or organize them in your department by getting a group of teachers involved and sharing instruction time.

- Schedule time in a computer lab (or extra time if it is a course with a computer component) for the class. Go through the steps of the computer skills you feel are most relevant for your course. For example, if using an electronic newsgroup, have students walk through the process of accessing, reading, and posting to the group. If you are insecure about teaching the procedure, enlist the help of a lab assistant. (Be certain to request such help when you schedule lab time. Don't surprise the lab attendant on the day of the presentation.)

- Build this extra computer-lab time into your syllabus; this avoids the problem of having to scrunch writing lessons in order to "fit" technology into the course.

- Provide students with simple, concise, written directions for performing the electronic processes important to the class.

- Be certain students understand the educational objective for the computer assignment.

- Incorporate into the class environment examples of successful/creative/productive uses of the required technology. If students have particularly insightful comments in the course newsgroup, for example, call attention to those postings and entice your audience by reading excerpts in class.

- Hold office hours in the computer lab and be available to answer procedural questions.

- Have technology tie into the regular classroom activities. Electronically post questions before a class discussion to get ideas flowing for in-class sharing of perspectives.

- Make the technology-produced portion of the class part of the grading scale. Be certain students understand the rubric applied.

Teaching in *any* forum requires enthusiasm for the subject matter and its delivery. A student's excitement for learning is enhanced by the instructor's energy. So don't *teach* the computer, but enjoy teaching *with* the technology that students will need to know in order to compete in the rapidly evolving world.

What to Expect from this Text

Planning any effective lesson involves first identifying the objective and then determining the most appropriate method for lesson delivery. The chapters in this text offer an overview of the various components of a writing course and strategies for presenting those objectives in a variety of electronic formats. Each individual activity includes a writing objective and a secondary technology goal that assist in focusing on the importance of the lesson to the overall course objectives.

Because each teaching situation varies according to class size, access to technology, teacher/student proficiency with technology, and quality of hardware, no two CMC courses will be identical. For this reason, we have provided a variety of strategies and activities ranging from plans to be used with stand-alone computers to designs for classes with high-end connections to a powerful campus infrastructure.

We have also anticipated that campuses have differing structures for integration of electronic media. Some classes meet every class period or at least once a week in the networked environment. Other courses are designed for blocks of lab time, perhaps a month-long period, that coincides with a project. Still another concept of integration involves using technology as supplemental, always outside of class time; students must use the lab at their convenience. We hope instructors in each of these teaching situations will be able to make use of the activities provided in the chapters that follow.

Conventions

This text discusses a number of specific computer applications and processes. To differentiate computer commands from other usages, we have written computer commands in CAPS. Web page addresses (URL's) are underlined and enclosed within angle brackets, as in <http://www.abacon.com>.

Words of Encouragement

Many of us moving into the electronic teaching space are hesitant to share what we are doing because we fear that we are doing it wrong--or not as brilliantly as others. This fear is common to most of us who begin the adventure of CMC. We hope this text will illustrate that there is no magic formula and no "right way" to approach teaching with technology. Neither can we provide a syllabus from which everyone can successfully teach an integrated composition course. Our goal is to provide ideas, activities, and encouragement to help educators create an integrated writing curriculum that fits the needs of their students. So one last bit of advice: enjoy the challenge! Your course will thrive from reevaluation and retooling, and your students will be better prepared for the writing challenges they face in the university and beyond.

Works Cited

Bollentin, Wendy Rickard. "Can Information Technology Improve Education: Measuring Voices, Attitudes and Perceptions." *Educom Review*. January/February 1998. 50-54.

Composing Cyberspace: Identity, Community, and Knowledge in the Electronic Age. Ed. Richard Holeton. Madison, WI: McGraw Hill, 1998. 415-425.

Facciola, Peter C. "Building an Effective Computer Learning Environment in the Dynamic Learning Classroom." *Syllabus*. 11.2 (1998). 12-14, 51.

Kay, Alan. "Computers, Networks and Education." 1995. *Literacy, Technology, and Society: Confronting the Issues*. Ed. Gail E. Hawisher and Cynthia L. Selfe. Upper Saddle River, NJ: Prentice Hall, 1997. 150-159.

Neill, Monty. "Computers, Thinking, and Schools in the 'New World Economic Order'." 1995.

Chapter 2

Some Guiding Principles

In this chapter, we will talk about five basic principles that enhance teaching in the electronic environment. These principles address some of the most common problems related to teaching writing with computers, and are designed to counteract those problems. This list is not designed to be inclusive, but rather, to point to a methodology of teaching conducive to the electronic environment (and, to some degree, to the traditional classroom as well):

- Integration
- Simplicity
- Consistency
- Preparation
- Improvisation

Integration

In many ways, the principle of Integration is most important. This principle indicates that every class should be focused on writing instruction, even when the class meets in a computer lab, even if the class doesn't get anything accomplished in the period except logging on to e-mail. The goal of every composition course is composition, not computer skills. Some teachers have a tendency to separate computer days from "traditional classroom" days, and even go so far as to list specific computer skills as the goal for that class. There is no faster path to failure. Computer skills must be integrated with writing goals or students will quickly see two things: 1) the teacher doesn't have the necessary knowledge to be teaching computers; and 2) computer days don't really matter, as there is no real writing instruction going on. We have presented these dangers polemically here, but it serves to make the point; technology in the classroom is a means to an end, a different set of media through which writing occurs. The work of the teacher is one of translation; that is, assuming the teacher knows what he or she wants to accomplish during a given class period in terms of writing goals, then the challenge is determining how to achieve those same goals using the electronic environment. The bulk of this book is designed to help the teacher through this translation process. The principle of Integration indicates that the translation must occur at some level, that the class remains centered on the instruction of writing regardless of the medium being used.

A second aspect of the principle of Integration, however, highlights the medium itself as a topic of discussion. Electronic communication is still a relative newborn compared to other communication technologies. Manuscript, print, and painted works of art are technologies that have been explored and discussed extensively; we know quite a bit about how and why each works from both scientific and philosophical perspectives. Even the somewhat newer technologies of telephone, cinema, and television have been explored and discussed over the past few decades and a large body of critical academic work has been devoted to these media. Electronic communication is less understood, partially because it is so new, and partially because the media change so very quickly. No sooner does one medium gain momentum and prestige than another comes along and supplants it. Currently, the World Wide Web seems to be the electronic medium of choice[1], and at the risk of pre-antiquation, it seems that the Web is going to stay around

---

[1] As we will discuss further in Chapter 7, the World Wide Web is actually an amalgam of media, and continues to grow and evolve on a regular basis.

for a while. Of course the Web itself is constantly changing, both in terms of form and function. An element of the Integration Principle indicates that these changes should be studied and examined, not simply used as if they worked in the same ways that print has worked historically. That is, while it is important to integrate the electronic media into the main writing goals of the course, it is also important to think about some of the differences each medium itself entails and implies. To return to the translation metaphor, any process of translation entails changes in the text itself because some things simply do not "translate" cleanly or easily. Such is certainly the case in other media -- anyone who has seen a movie version of "Dracula" will note massive differences between the movie and printed versions of Stoker's original text, in part due to the nature of the media. Such differences also occur when translating into electronic media, and it is important for teachers and students to be cognizant of these differences.

A third aspect of the Integration principle concerns the level of computer integration the class employs. Think of computer use on a sliding scale. On one end, we have classes with minimal computer integration, where the teacher runs the classroom basically as a traditional classroom, and makes only occasional use of the computer. On the other end of the scale, we have classes with complete computer integration, such as an on-line course, where the electronic environment provides the only medium of discussion and pedagogy. Most courses will fall somewhere between these two poles, using computers heavily for some lessons or projects and less for others. An important point to keep in mind is to remain flexible in terms of the amount of integration your class uses. It is perfectly acceptable to design a lesson in the computer room that entails students turning off their computer screens and turning around for an oral class discussion. Conversely, it is perfectly acceptable to conduct class discussion using e-mail or newsgroups. The amount and kinds of computer integration should be determined by the kinds of writing goals being pursued, and the relative comfort of the teacher and students with different elements of the electronic environment. Teachers must also consider the availability to students of the relied upon technologies; some campus have limited facilities, inadequate equipment, and inaccessible lab hours that students must contend with when attempting to complete assignments.

Simplicity

The principle of Simplicity is not new to the teaching of writing, and is more popularly called Ockham's Razor ("the easiest explanation is usually the correct one," or "don't make it more complicated than it has to be"). Simply put, this principle says that if there is a simple way to accomplish something, then that is usually the best way to proceed. This principle is especially important in an electronic environment.

One of the most important considerations of teaching in a computer lab is the amount of class time that will be occupied with computer instruction as such. That is, although the class is a writing class and activities will be geared toward that end, some class time will almost always need to be devoted to computer instructions dealing with issues such as turning the machines on, opening up and using the word processor, setting up and using e-mail, or getting onto the World Wide Web. One of the most important goals for the teacher, then, is to minimize the amount of time spent teaching computers, and to maximize the amount of time spent teaching writing.

The principle of Simplicity speaks directly to this issue, and manifests itself in a few different ways. First, when deciding on which program to use for any given activity, choose the one easiest for students to use. As time goes on, fancy commercial programs (such as Microsoft Word or Internet Explorer) get bigger as new features are added, and more options are provided for the user. According to this principle, however, bigger is not necessarily better, because the newer, fancier programs can provide too many options, and confuse students. Often, smaller programs (such as Notepad, Write, or Mosaic) are easier to use because they are relatively uncluttered. In some cases, these smaller, simpler programs work fine for classroom purposes, and take up far less class time than do their full-featured counterparts.

Second, the principle of Simplicity indicates that it is usually better to use one program than two. Assuming that introducing each program used in class will take up some small amount of class time, teachers will want to minimize the number of different programs they use. Thus, it is better to use one full-featured program than two simpler programs. The net time spent teaching the students how to work in the program will be decreased if they can stay in one environment for most or all of their activities. Ultimately, teachers want to find a single program that serves all of their class needs. Such programs do exist and developers are working on ways to make these kinds of integrated writing and teaching environments easier to use and more accessible via the World Wide Web. In some ways, this second point might seem to contradict the first, but the principle of Simplicity is a balancing act to find the easiest and least time-consuming environment that facilitates class activities.

Consistency

The principle of Consistency works off that of Simplicity and indicates that whatever program(s) the teacher ends up choosing for class work, the class should use that program and method consistently. That is, using any computer program in class comes down to a finite number of discrete steps (1. Turn on computer; 2. Open up a Word processor; 3. Open new document; 4. Write the assignment; 5. Save the assignment; 6. Print the assignment). Teachers should work on making these steps consistent from class period to class period so that students will begin to perform the steps automatically; the automation of technical information allows students to concentrate on writing instead of on how to use the computer. In this respect, repetition is the teacher's ally, and the teacher should try to design exercises that use the same series of steps as much as possible.

Of course, the instructor may want to integrate different kinds of procedures or programs throughout the semester; the principle of Consistency would advise teachers to make such changes slowly and gradually, making sure students became used to one set of procedures before others are introduced. This principle also advises teachers to explain new programs or procedures in a consistent fashion. For example, when a teacher first introduces a program, he or she may want to supply students a simple printed handout that outlines the computer steps students will perform. When the teacher switches to a new program or uses another aspect of the old program (the latter encouraging Simplicity), he or she may want to use the same kind of printed handout to introduce the new component.

This principle is hardly unique to teaching in the electronic environment, but it is especially important here in terms of maximizing the amount of writing instruction, and minimizing the amount of computer instruction. Teachers who try to use four different programs in the first month of class will usually find that their students have learned none of the programs and are likely very frustrated by their experience with computers. Even those students familiar with computers can find this jumping around confusing and frustrating -- students who are not used to computers usually start to panic even more quickly. Teachers who stick with one program and use that program in a variety of ways find that their students are much more productive and more comfortable in the writing space.

Preparation

The principle of Preparation contains two distinct elements, and each is important for a successful class experience.

First, the Preparation Principle concerns "plan B," a backup-plan in the event that the computers do not work for whatever reason. Normally, this "plan B" will be a lesson plan teachers can use in a traditional classroom, but taking into consideration two additional elements. The class is now in a computer room, whose architecture may or may not be conducive to traditional teaching procedures. Teachers should determine, before the class, if there is a traditional classroom available and accessible should this kind of meltdown occur. Teachers must also remember that some portion of the class period has been taken up determining that the computers will not, in fact, operate. If it takes more than 15 or 20 minutes for the class to open the main application, then the teacher should move to "plan B" and salvage as much instruction as possible out of the remaining class time. Preferably, teachers will double-check the lab and computers before class to make sure everything is operational.

The second (and hopefully the more prevalent) use of the Preparation Principle concerns the amount and kind of preparation teachers need to perform before class time. As a rule, classes in the electronic classroom require more preparation than do classes in a traditional classroom. Further, this preparation depends upon the relative level of computer integration used in the class. Lessons with minimal computer integration will require only a small amount of extra preparation, while fully on-line courses require large amounts of preparation time. One of the most interesting and beneficial aspects of teaching in the electronic environment concerns the relative independence afforded students. Fully, or even mostly, on-line courses are usually designed so that students have some autonomy in terms of how long they need to finish any particular piece of the assignment. Accordingly, teachers who use this sort of approach need to have the different elements of the assignment in place before the beginning of class to accommodate individual learning styles.

The preparation time involved in designing a course is very intensive the first time the course is taught. This is especially true for courses that integrate technology into the delivery mechanisms. Conversely, the second or third time a traditional course is taught, teachers find that their overall preparation time decreases as they become accustomed to the kinds of exercises that are successful. This decrease is even more marked when using technology because the activities are already done (on disk, posted to the Web, saved in a central location), and the main jobs of the teacher become modification and customization.

This book is designed to minimize the amount of initial preparation time required of teachers new to the electronic environment by suggesting specific lesson plans and activities for composition courses. Of course, teachers are encouraged to modify lessons or use the activities described herein as springboards for their own class activities. Our hope is to provide teachers a series of templates and a running start toward successful use of technology in the composition classroom.

Improvisation

The final principle of successful teaching in an electronic environment is that of Improvisation. Certainly, experienced teachers will be familiar with this idea; many traditional classroom activities need to be modified "on the fly," as teachers realize that the day's activities are not working as anticipated. This principle is especially important when teaching in the computer classroom, and applies in a couple of different respects.

The first aspect of the Preparation Principle discusses the need for teachers to have a "plan B" in the event that the computer lab crashes, or is inoperable for whatever reason. Though this unfortunate situation does come to pass from time to time, it is much more common that the computers will work, more or less, and it is this "more or less" that the Principle of Improvisation concerns. Say, for example, the class activity involves groups logging on to a computer with an Internet connection, and from there, visiting an on-line grammar site posted to the World Wide Web. In the process of going through the activity, the teacher realizes with utter dismay that although the computers seem to be working fine, the site in question has "vanished." According to the Principle of Improvisation, instead of abandoning the lesson for the day, the teacher might ask the students to go to an alternate grammar site which, being familiar with the Principle of Preparation, the teacher has located before class. Alternately, the teacher may ask students to do an Internet search, and find a grammar site on their own. Of course, the teacher may simply ask the students to pull out their trusty printed grammar handbooks and perform that portion of the day's activities manually.

The Improvisation Principle generally suggests that if some of the components of a lesson or activity do not work, then use the components that do work in creative ways. One special scenario that we should mention here involves multi-tasking, that is, running more than one application at the same time. Sometimes, particularly on older or slower computers, running more than one application (especially large or memory-intensive applications such as Microsoft Word, Netscape Communicator, PowerPoint, or Excel) can cause very slow operations, or even system failures or malfunctions. Though the Simplicity Principle suggests avoidance of heavy multi-tasking, there may be lessons or activities in which the simultaneous use of several programs is preferable or unavoidable. In this scenario, assuming that systems or computer speeds become sufficiently problematic, the Improvisation Principle recommends that the teachers finds another route to their goals, such as using a smaller version of one of the programs, or exiting one large application before launching a second.

(Troubleshooting Experience)

An additional trait of the computer lab veteran is the ability to troubleshoot some minor technical problems. Truly, the job and expertise of the teacher should be in writing instruction, not computer savvy. Nevertheless, the teacher most successful in the electronic environment will be one able to fix some minor problems on her own, without needing to wait for a lab or technical assistant. The kinds of problems we are discussing here are the typical user-related problems common to teaching in a computer lab, such as saving correctly, reading or sending e-mail, or accessing the correct Internet site. Largely, this knowledge is a function of experience; as teachers become familiar with the computer labs and see the same problems occur many times, they learn solutions. There are two other very useful sources of information about this kind of basic troubleshooting. First, a huge repository of information can be found on the Internet, through Web pages, newsgroups, mailing lists, and other archive databases. These can be laborious to look through, but chances are very good that the answer is out there. A second, and probably more useful, source of information, is found in the practical experience of peers or even students who have run across the problem before and know how to fix it. Most "techie" communities are overjoyed at the opportunity to display their knowledge and help someone out, and teachers should make use of this resource as much as possible. Nothing replaces sharing information with colleagues, students, and lab personnel. Frequently, when users share information about lab problems, patterns begin to develop that help trace the root of the problem. Whenever possible, teachers should report problems to the lab staff immediately after class. Experienced teachers can help technicians solve problems by recording the steps that led to the problem and any error messages. The more information the technicians possess, the more quickly they can identify and resolve the problem.

These five main principles are not written in stone, nor do they guarantee success; they are guidelines to help teachers think about the kinds of issues they will be facing in class, and suggestions on how to avoid some of the most common kinds of mistakes teachers unwittingly make in the electronic environment. The principles work collectively, and cross lines frequently; to follow one principle leads to consideration of others, and the design of any particular class assignment often takes all five into account.

Chapter 3

Word-Processing Basics

The most important software for teaching a composition class is the word processor. Simply put, a word processor is a program designed to produce printable text documents, though many recent word-processing packages can do much more, such as tables, graphs, images, and even hyper-linked annotations within a document. Undoubtedly, students will use the word processor heavily on a day-to-day basis for in-class writing and other activities; to encourage technology use, many instructors require final papers to be word-processed. In this text, we are assuming some familiarity with basic word-processing, but this chapter will go over some of the functions that are important in terms of teaching a composition class, and some important issues that instructors need to think about. It is one thing to perform relatively complex operations (such as using hyper-links or images in a word-processing document) for our own work; it is another thing entirely to teach students how to perform these operations in a classroom setting. In this chapter, we will cover:

- Issues in choosing a word processor for class
- How to save, rename, and change file types
- How to CUT, COPY, and PASTE
- Using FIND/REPLACE

Word Processor Types

There are two general kinds of word processors: the full-featured word-processing suite, and the basic bare-bones word processor (the bare-bones processor usually comes pre-installed with the operating system: Windows, Mac OS, etc.). Different word processors perform different functions and each has a set of strengths and liabilities; instructors need to be aware of these properties and choose the word processor most appropriate for the situation. Even if the university has a standard full-featured word-processing package, instructors must choose which *kind* of word processor to use for particular class exercises.

The Full-Featured Word Processor

The full-featured word-processing suite is the deluxe model of the word processor. These programs, such as Microsoft Word and Corel WordPerfect, are full-function programs loaded with accessories. The most recent releases of both Word and WordPerfect can perform an amazing range of activities: spell- and grammar-checking are performed automatically; users can insert tables, graphs, images, even sounds and movies; users can save and publish their documents as Web pages; even the toolbars can be customized.

<u>Advantages of the Full-Featured Word Processor</u>

The advantages of this kind of a program lie in the breadth of activities it can perform and the ease of writing, revising, and publishing documents. In addition, most recent word-processing suites have excellent file translation libraries that open documents written in different programs while preserving the formatting of the original text. Considering these advantages, the full-featured word processor is appropriate for final papers or writing assignments that make use of some special features that these programs offer, such as inserting images, using footnotes, or creating tables and graphs.

A secondary advantage of the full-featured word processor involves its carry-over value. A valid argument for the incorporation of technology into the classroom rests on the fact that students need a certain amount of techno-literacy to be competitive in today's marketplace. While the composition class is primarily focused on writing and not computers, students nevertheless gain valuable knowledge and experience insofar as the computer skills they learn and use in their composition class carry over to other classes or to marketable job skills in the workplace.

Disadvantages of the Full-Featured Word Processor

There are, however, two main disadvantages to the full-featured word processor. First, there are sometimes *too many* options. For example, if a student wants to insert an endnote or change the spacing of a paragraph, there may not be an obvious way for her to do so. The sheer number of options and functions within the program can often be confusing and discouraging, and students can waste prodigious amounts of time trying to figure out functions in the program itself. The point of the course is to teach writing, not to teach computers or the complexity of modern word processors; classes should avoid functions that will take up an undue amount of time and effort.

Second, in order to include all of these wonderful options and functions, full-featured word-processing suites are normally HUGE (sometimes in excess of 60 megabytes), and getting bigger with each new release. If the class is working on older computers, or running programs off a network, this issue of size can create problems ranging from mild inconvenience to total meltdown. On older computers, some programs may not run if the computer does not meet the minimum requirements of the program. If the computer barely meets these minimums the program will run, but will probably be very slow and may cause problems (such as freezing when saving or printing). Teachers should check with the lab administrator about running applications in the lab and then **test** the word processors in the electronic classroom before the beginning of the semester to make sure they work adequately. If possible, teachers should try to check the environment with a full complement of users to ensure that the programs will run as expected with a whole class working simultaneously.

The Bare-Bones Word Processor

The second, and usually overlooked (at least in terms of pedagogy) kind of word processor is the basic, bare-bones kind of program, such as Microsoft's Notepad, Microsoft's WordPad, or Macintosh's Simpletext. These word processors do not have many of the capabilities of their full-featured kin, and therein lie both their main strength and main weakness.

Disadvantages of the Bare-Bones Word Processor

In terms of liabilities, these kinds of word processors usually cannot perform any special formatting functions, such as tables or charts. Most cannot translate other file types accurately; either they will not open a document at all, or the document will be loaded with gibberish characters (see Appendix D for more information). They certainly cannot use images, make or read hypertext, or use a grammar checker. Some may not even allow the creation of footnotes, headers and footers, or even spell-check. If course assignments require any of these functions, then teachers should opt for a full-functioned word processor.

Advantages of the Bare-Bones Word Processor

On the plus side, however, the bare-bones word processor is perfectly adequate for most informal writing assignments. Students can type, save, print, use simple formatting such as bold, italic, and underline, and perhaps even use some slightly more complex features (variable font type and size, special characters or bullets, saving as a different file type). If assignments do not require any special formatting, then a smaller word processor may be the more appropriate choice; the layout is typically less confusing, and students may feel more comfortable in this less intimidating environment.

A second, and perhaps more important, advantage to this kind of word processor is its small size. Almost regardless of hardware, the smaller streamlined word processor will open more quickly and operate more effectively than a full-featured program; there is simply much less to go wrong. This consideration may be very important depending on the hardware in the electronic classroom. If full-featured programs operate slowly or create problems, then consider using the smaller word processor.

Even if the full-featured program runs well in the electronic classroom, there are certain situations in which the smaller program is preferable, such as heavy in-class multi-tasking. Multi-tasking is when users have multiple programs, documents, or windows open at a time, and switch back and forth among them. This scenario frequently occurs in composition classes when students are asked to switch between a World Wide Web browser (such as Netscape, Mosaic, or Internet Explorer) and a word-processing window. When multi-tasking, remember that every open program claims a certain amount of memory (RAM), and the bigger the program, the more memory it will claim for itself. Thus, while a Word program might run fine by itself, when multi-tasked with a Web browser, it might run very slowly or may not open at all.

Choosing a Word Processor

In general, the full-featured word processor is more appropriate for final drafts or assignments that require special formatting features, but can be confusing and may cause delays or complications because of its size and complexity. The bare-bones word processor is more appropriate for small or informal writing assignments. The instructor's choice should be based on the kinds of assignments students need to write as well as the capabilities of the hardware in the classroom. Often, instructors end up choosing one of each: a full-featured word processor for final papers and assignments which require special formatting, and a bare-bones word processor for most in-class writing assignments. Instructors who choose both kinds of programs in this way spend class time familiarizing students only with the full-featured word processor, working under the reasonable assumption that if students can operate the more complex program, they can also operate the simple program.

Word-Processing Standardization

After deciding which kind of the word processor(s) to use, instructors have one more important word-processing choice. Many students have their own computers and word processors and will ask if they can use their own programs to write their papers. The advantage to allowing them to use their own programs is that they will probably be familiar with them, and may be more comfortable writing in those environments. A serious disadvantage to allowing this option is that the student's word processor may not be compatible with the word processor used in class. Incompatibility causes serious complications when students take their documents from lab to a home computer and back to lab.

Instructors may want to consider requiring a standard word processor. If everyone is using the same program, then opening documents is not a problem because they are all saved in the same format. Teaching special formatting features is also much easier, as the processes are precisely the same for everyone. Unfortunately, many word-processing programs are very expensive, and it may not be realistic to expect everyone to invest in new programs for your class (word-processing suites such as Microsoft Office can run into hundreds of dollars). Eventually, most instructors end up requiring operating knowledge of a primary word-processing program, but allow students to use their own as well, so long as the students are comfortable with both, understand how to perform any necessary file translations on their own, and recognize that they are responsible for the integrity and accessibility of their texts. We recommend that all final papers be saved in the format of the word processor the class will be using to help cut down on the number of translation and printing problems at the end of the semester.

Saving

Regardless of the instructor's word processor decisions, the most important word-processing function used in the class will be saving a document. This is a good time to reiterate the first golden rule of doing anything on computers: save early, save often. We have seen first-hand many examples of a student's in-class writing essay disappearing with a power surge, lab malfunction, or user error. It is especially important to save before printing, as systems often experience printing problems that result in a frozen system and loss of unsaved data.

In most word processors, documents can be saved in two ways. First, when performing the SAVE option, typically located under the FILE menu, the word processor will automatically save the document, writing over the old document. Second, using a SAVE AS option, also typically located in the FILE menu (usually right below SAVE), users can re-name a document, change the destination to which the file will be saved, or even change the file type of the document. Figure 3-1 shows a screenshot of a SAVE AS Dialogue screen, and Figure 3-2 summarizes the functions of each of these options. Instructors should make sure each student is familiar with these SAVE and SAVE AS functions, devoting class time to the procedure if necessary. The quickest way for anyone to be turned off technology is to lose hours worth of work because of a saving error.

Word-Processing Basics

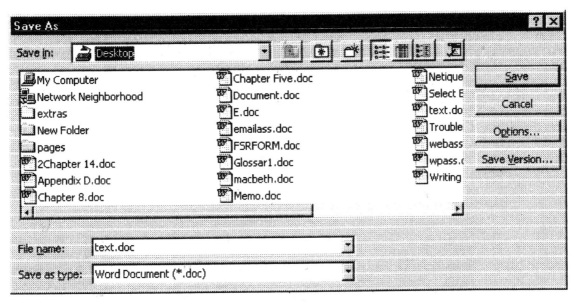

Figure 3-1: SAVE AS Dialogue Window[2]

	SAVE	**SAVE AS**
How to …	• Click FILE, select SAVE • Save button (Floppy Disk Icon – usually in top left hand corner) • Ctrl + S (keystroke shortcut) • Auto-save[3]	• Click FILE, select SAVE AS • SAVE new document[4]
Action	• Replaces older version of document with current version	• Opens SAVE AS DIALOGUE BOX
Options (DIALOGUE BOX)	• None.	• Save In (location): Change the location of the file[5] • File Name: Change the name of the file[6] • File Type: Change the *kind* of file to be saved[7]

---

[2] Screen shot reprinted by permission from Microsoft Corporation

[3] Most full-featured word-processors come equipped with an auto-save function that automatically saves the document at prescribed intervals without user invention (check with the lab administrator to see if the word-processor has an auto-save function, and how it is configured).

[4] When working on a new document (which will typically be named "untitled *x*" or "document *x*"), the first time a user SAVES the document, they will be presented with the SAVE AS DIALOGUE screen, which will ask the user to supply a name for the document, and where to save it. Thereafter, every time "SAVE" is selected, the document will overwrite the older version with the newer.

[5] To save to a floppy disk on a typical Windows system, save to the A: drive. To save to a floppy disk on a typical Macintosh system, click on Desktop in the right-hand portion of the dialogue screen, and then double-click on the floppy disk icon that appears in the right hand screen.

[6] When re-naming, do NOT type in a different file extension (usually the three letters at the end of a file name; for example, "document1.doc" or "untitled.wpd"). Doing so will only confuse the computer and make the file unreadable. To change the file type, users MUST change the FILE TYPE option in the SAVE AS dialogue box.

[7] For additional information on using different file types, see Appendix D.

	SAVE	**SAVE AS**
When to use	• Saving changes to open documents • Periodic saving to prevent data loss	• Save changes as new file name to preserve original document. • Change file location (usually from floppy disk to hard drive or *vice versa*) • Change file format to ensure readability at home, in class.

Figure 3-2: SAVE and SAVE AS

Apart from these basic saving functions, instructors should consider two additional issues: standardized naming protocols and translation accessibility. First, instructors may want to consider supplying students with a standard format to use when saving class documents, particularly if students hand in assignments electronically or on disk. This rubric should avoid unduly long file names; while some systems can read long file names, others cannot, resulting in translation difficulties. Further, long file names tend to make file organization problematic, as some screens (such as on OPEN FILE dialogue box) will display only the first few characters of the file. Instead, try to use short descriptive names, putting important naming information first (for example, "a3lastname" for assignment number 3; "fp4lastname" for final paper number 4, or "initialsdate" are all easy and effective naming systems). Second, in terms of translatability, we again recommend that the instructor require all homework assignments and final papers be saved in the file format of the main class word processor.

One special format option is SAVE AS HTML, available in some newer full-featured word-processing suites. If files are saved as HTML, the documents will be formatted as Web pages, which means that they can be opened up and viewed (but not

---

[6] For additional information on using different file types, see Appendix D.

edited) in any Web browser, such as Netscape Navigator or Internet Explorer.[7] This option makes the creation of Web documents easier than ever -- but teachers should be aware that most other word processors cannot read an HTML document.

Ensure File Translatability through Redundant File Saves

If instructors or students are unsure of which file type to SAVE AS, we recommend saving three versions of the document to ensure that one will be readable. Save one copy in the program's default file type (.doc for a Microsoft Word document, .wpd for a WordPerfect document), one in rich-text format (.rtf), and one in ASCII or text-only format (.txt). The program's default file type will save the document the most accurately, preserving the formatting exactly, but other word processors may have trouble opening the document. Saving as text-only will preserve very little of the original formatting (even formatting like italics or underlining will be lost), but any word processor, regardless of size or age, will be able to open the file. Rich-text format is a good middle ground; it will preserve most of the formatting, and will be compatible with a large number of word processors.

CUT, COPY, and PASTE

CUT, COPY, and PASTE are probably the three most used, least appreciated, functions of modern computers. These tools facilitate moving text around in a single document, between documents, or even between different programs with a few simple keystrokes. COPY and PASTE can be especially useful in terms of copying Web

---

[7] By definition, Web browsers can only read HTML documents. The most popular browsers include an integrated HTML editor (Netscape Composer, and Microsoft Frontpage, respectively) as well, but these elements are separate and work in different ways.

addresses or other text strings that demand exact syntax. Figure 3-3 summarizes the main operations of these functions.

	CUT	COPY	PASTE
How to...	1. Highlight (Select) text 2. Click the EDIT menu, then select CUT	1. Highlight (Select) text 2. Click the EDIT menu, then select COPY	1. Move cursor to desired insertion point 2. Click the EDIT menu, then select PASTE
Keystroke Shortcuts[8]	• Ctrl + X • (open apple + X for Mac)	• Ctrl + C • (Open apple + C for Mac)	• Ctrl + V • (Open apple + V for Mac)
Action	• Copies highlighted text into clipboard, removing original from document.	• Copies highlighted text into clipboard, preserving original in document.	• Inserts contents of clipboard at insertion point.
When to use	• Moving text around within a document.	• Moving text between documents • Copying text from a read-only document (like a Web page or a CD-ROM) • Copying special characters • Copying Web addresses or other syntax specific text-strings	• Pasting text or images into an open document • Pasting Web addresses into a browser • Pasting special characters • Pasting common or frequent character strings

Figure 3-3: CUT, COPY, and PASTE

When users COPY or CUT text, they are actually storing the highlighted text in an invisible file called a "clipboard." The clipboard is simply a virtual storage bin that holds the text in question until the user is ready to PASTE it into a new document. The writer cannot normally edit information in the clipboard -- it simply allows data to be moved from one place to another. The clipboard retains the highlighted text until it is

---

[8] Keystroke shortcuts are especially useful for CUT, COPY, and PASTE. First, keystrokes are eventually faster than mouse commands, so facilitate uninterrupted composition. Second and perhaps more importantly, these keystrokes will almost always work, even if a window does not present an EDIT menu. If you can highlight text, you can COPY it; if you can enter text, you can PASTE.

CLEARED (a function found in the EDIT menu), OR until something else is COPIED or CUT. In other words, the clipboard can store only one data set at a time, whether that data set is a single word or a ten-page essay.

COPY and PASTE are basic computer skills that all students should know, so it's worth taking some time at the beginning of the term to make sure everyone is familiar with the process. Many teachers incorporate these skills into their daily routine, having students COPY daily assignments or quizzes from a central file (perhaps the class Webpage) to the word processor on their computers, there to be edited or completed.

Find/Replace

One special use of COPY and PASTE involves the FIND/REPLACE functions included in most word processors. The FIND and REPLACE commands, usually located within the EDIT menu, facilitate quickly editing a text by finding or replacing individual characters or long character strings within the body of a text. For example, a student hands in a draft in which she has consistently misspelled the name of your textbook. Instead of manually going through every instance and changing each separately, the student could use the FIND/REPLACE function to find and change all of them at the same time (using a GLOBAL REPLACE option). COPY and PASTE are particularly useful here, because the student can simply COPY the incorrect text and PASTE it into the FIND/REPLACE dialogue screen, and then type in the corrected version, and select REPLACE ALL. Note, however, that the FIND/REPLACE dialogue screen will normally not provide an EDIT menu, so the student will have to use the keystroke shortcuts in order to PASTE in the search string (see Figure 3-3). This function of COPY and PASTE is especially useful when replacing special characters, such as international characters (ó, ë) or other symbols (©, @), which cannot be typed into the FIND/REPLACE dialogue box. Figure 3-4 shows a sample of a FIND/REPLACE dialogue screen.

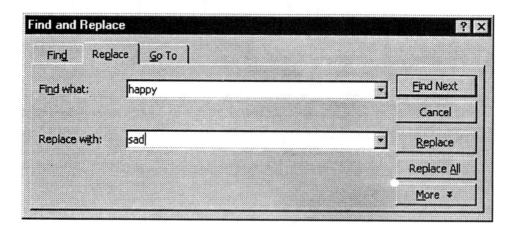

Figure 3-4: FIND/REPLACE Dialogue Window

Spell Check/ Grammar Check

Spell and grammar checkers are easy to use, and recent versions of both Microsoft Word and Corel WordPerfect offer suggestions on the fly (that is, as the user types, without requiring a separate "Spell Check" action). Teachers, however, need to be wary of these tools. Spell checkers only determine whether or not words are in their internal dictionaries and will not highlight words spelled correctly but used in the wrong context (*they're* instead of *their*). We need to remind our students that spell check is not a substitute for good proofreading; it is at best a supplement to that process.

Grammar checkers are even more problematic, and many teachers recommend their students not use grammar checkers at all. Grammar checkers often offer inappropriate or incorrect grammar suggestions, and unless the writer is experienced enough to know when to take advice and when to ignore it, the grammar checker can actually hurt the paper. Grammar checkers can be useful for pointing out such writing habits as passive voice, but again, students need to use caution in accepting the provided corrections. In any case, teachers need to explain the correct use of these tools to students, and urge caution in their use. Above all, we must emphasize the need for good manual proofreading as the only sure way to copyedit any text.

Using Help

Most modern word processors (even bare-bones) come with decent Help documentation. On a Windows system, users can find help under the Help menu. On a Macintosh system (MacOS 7.0 or greater), help is located in the Balloon Menu (top right-hand corner, denoted by a question mark). Normally, users can browse through the Help file either by topic (through a table of contents), or through a searchable keyword index. If users are looking for general information, the content/topic method is the more effective procedure; if users are looking for specific instructions or directions, then the searchable keyword index is usually more effective.

Guiding students to and through the help files should be an early activity or homework assignment in the class. If students know how to look for and use Help files themselves, and are responsible for doing so, then the class will run more smoothly and the instructor will be saved many headaches. Here is a small sample assignment the class could use to become familiarized with Help:

Sample Assignment: Using Help (in any full-featured word processor)
1. How do you access the Help menu?
2. What does the help menu say about creating columns in the document?
3. How do you change indentation for a single paragraph?
4. How do you save your document in Rich Text Format?
5. How do you create and edit tables?

Figure 3-5: Sample Assignment using HELP

Chapter 4

Using the Word Processor in Class

One of the earliest pieces of advice (warnings) given to teachers who use an electronic environment is: "Don't just use the computer as a glorified typewriter." Administrators and composition-technology theorists alike want something more out of the electronic environment than a place where students can type their papers and print out legible copies. The word processor creates a space for writing, and this space is more useful to the composition class in its support for the writing process than in its ability to create polished printed documents. Word processors make every text an eminently revisable one, and courses that meet in or have access to a computer lab find that the electronic writing space itself is conducive to a process-approach of teaching writing.

One huge advantage of the word processor is that it is relatively self-sufficient. Even a bare-bones word-processing application can be a very useful and functional environment for programs that do not have more advanced technologies such as Internet capability or fast new computers. Even those programs that possess very high-end technology can find a number of useful pedagogical functions in the word processor. In this chapter, we will discuss some of the different kinds of ways the word processor can be used in the composition course. More specifically, we will discuss the word processor as:

- a writing space
- a revision toolbox
- a medium of collaboration
- a desktop publisher
- a virtual classroom (with a Local Area Network)

The Word Processor as Writing Space

Perhaps, like the calculator, the word processor has become so commonplace, so expected, that many people fail to appreciate just how useful it is and subsequently overlook some of the potential value of the tool. Certainly, the word processor is useful as a space for drafting and revision. In this respect, the word processor really is a new and improved typewriter. Once the program is open, users can usually begin typing on a new blank document, or open up an existing document to continue working or revising.

The writing space itself is surely the most obvious and frequently used aspect of the word processor. In this writing space, students can immediately begin to compose, clearly a valuable activity in a composition course. In addition, word processors offer users a number of tools that teachers can employ creatively. For example, nearly all word processors offer a variety of fonts and font sizes; a creative teacher might use such a tool in a number of ways. If the student is working on producing dialogue, the teacher might ask the student to pick a different font for each character, reinforcing the idea that each character has a distinctive voice. Further, the teacher might ask the student to base this choice of font on the personality of the character involved, forcing the student to think about the relationship between form and content in the text.

The word processor as writing space can also be used for a variety of pre-writing activities. One such activity, known as "blind writing," involves students opening up the word processor, but then turning off the screen (monitor) so that they cannot see what they are writing. The students then free-write without the recursive nuisance of watching their text unfold. Of course, the word processor works well for any kind of free-writing, even for those students who haven't taken "keyboarding" courses. If nothing else, this kind of free-writing activity accomplishes two things: it gets students into "writing mode" and it provides keyboarding practice. Like the writing process itself, keyboarding is a skill that improves with practice, and the word processor is a wonderful space for nurturing both these activities. Free-writing at the computer also encourages students to move to "terminal composition"--a term we coined to describe writing directly to the computer without the intermediate step of pencil and paper. When students become comfortable with free-writing on the computer, they are more likely to adapt to terminal composition as a writing method, a step that saves time and allows more opportunities for revision.

The basic writing space of full-featured word processors adds a number of other kinds of tools and tricks. Students may be able to colorize text, add clip-art or other kinds of images, create tables and graphs, even create an index or glossary to their papers. One obvious application of some of these more advanced features might include having students use the BULLET or NUMBERED LIST function of their word processors to create a structured outline or paper prospectus.

The Word Processor as Revision Toolbox

If the most obvious function of a word processor is as a space for writing, the next most obvious and frequent use is for a space of re-writing. All word processors contain tools useful to the revision process, and this usefulness pertains to two "levels" or kinds of revision.

First, on a superficial and somewhat problematic level, are spell-checking and grammar-checking tools. These functions can be useful, but are more often dangerously abused and misused by students. Some newer word processors include very intrusive spell-checking functions that can "correct" certain kinds of mistakes (capitalizing the first letter of a sentence and correcting letter reversal such as "and" for "and") AUTOMATICALLY! In some cases, users might want to type some of these "mistakes" on purpose, and the automatic spell-check can cause serious errors as it starts correcting what it perceives to be mistakes. This option can be turned off, but only if the user knows it is on in the first place. On the whole, these functions are useful, if perhaps too aggressively convenient, but teachers should be careful to discuss these tools with their classes.

In addition to its value as a basic writing space, the word processor is very useful for exercises concerning writing mechanics. For example, a teacher might present students with a block of text without paragraph breaks, have the student insert those breaks, and perhaps defend their choices. Many teachers use a similar assignment for punctuation; they give students unpunctuated or incorrectly punctuated sentences or paragraphs, and have the students correct or supply the correct punctuation. Teachers might copy a sentence from each student paper and have the class edit problematic prose from their own work. This works especially well if papers are handed in electronically; teachers can then COPY and PASTE sentences from students' work into an activity document. These ideas may seem very similar to the kind of exercises you might find in a writing workbook, because in a way, the word processor offers the space of a potential writing workbook. Students can write in it easily, can turn in exercises easily (by printing them out), and can save each exercise for future reference. Teachers should be encouraged to experiment with this workbook aspect of the word processor, because its potential uses are almost unlimited.

On a more global level of revision, the CUT, COPY, and PASTE functions of word processors are uniquely appropriate to revision exercises that concern document structure, paragraphing, organization, and ordering. Some teachers integrate these functions by presenting students with a document in which the paragraphs have been all mixed up; students are asked to rearrange the paragraphs in correct sequence, and perhaps write a justification of their arrangement. A more immediately practical variation of this exercise might ask students to rearrange the points in their own papers, and reflect on the differences alternate organizations make to their argument as a whole.

A last element of the word processor as Revision Toolbox is a reminder of the SAVE AS capability. That is, when students revise a draft, they can preserve the original by saving the revision under a slightly different name (adding a "2" or "3" to the front of the filename is an easy rubric). When the student finishes each set of revisions, she can save each under a different file name, creating a document history that preserves the kinds of changes that occurred along the way. This "paper trail" can be particularly useful for classes that emphasize the writing process, and is also an easy way to prevent, or at least discourage, plagiarism.

The Word Processor as a Medium of Collaboration

Though e-mail is the more useful medium for electronic class discussion and collaboration, the word processor does offer some collaborative techniques. High-end full-featured word processors may include fancy methods of collaboration, such as the ability to hyperlink text (link one part of a document to another part of the same document or a different document). Even bare-bones word processors can be effectively used by the creative teacher to enhance writing through collaboration. For example, every word processor can save information to disk. A simple collaborative assignment might ask students to switch disks, open a specified paper, and comment on that paper (possibly using a different font to specify peer remarks or suggestions in the paper). Instead of swapping disks, students could simply swap computers (i.e., change seats) for the same effect. A variation of this assignment might ask to student to "play phone" with the computers. In this exercise, students would write one sentence in a word processor, and then move one chair to the left. They would write the second sentence of THAT story, then move to the left again. At the end of the exercise, you would have one complete story per student, and every student would have written a portion of every story. This kind of exercise is often entertaining, and is a good way to build collaborative writing communities.

Another simple collaborative potential of even the bare-bones word processor involves group work with the computer as the focal point. In many writing classes, teachers assume that each student will be sitting and writing at his or her own computer. While this scenario is often useful, teachers should not allow themselves to feel trapped by the computers. Students can be arranged into pairs or larger groups around each computer and participate in group activities as in the traditional classroom. The computers provide an easy and effective writing space; creative groups might assign different fonts to identify group members in any particular activity. Similarly, using

CUT and PASTE, a group might easily combine several separate documents into a single file, and work on editing the composite file as a polished collaborative document.

Newer full-featured word processors may offer other kinds of collaborative opportunities. Some word processors offer the ability to add special comments or glosses into an existing text that are visually separated from the original document. These functions are normally located within the INSERT menu, and allow multiple users to add distinct commentary and feedback in a single document. In addition, more and more word processors allow hyperlinks to be embedded within the text, allowing a reader who clicks on the designated word or phrase to be sent to the appropriate location, usually a page on the World Wide Web. In addition, specialty software applications exist that are designed to "extend" the capabilities of the word processor. Some of these applications allow students to send word-processing files across the Internet to other students or teachers while others facilitate a truly collaborative environment whereby multiple students can simultaneously work on the same document.

The Word Processor as a Desktop Publisher

In addition to its value as a space of primary composition and of revision, the word processor offers a range of publishing capabilities. The most obvious of these capabilities (and the most often abused, some might suggest) is simple printing. Normally, anything that can be put into a word processor can be printed out. Most modern word processors are WYSIWYG (What You See Is What You Get) applications. Again, most modern users may take this kind of interface for granted, but not so many years ago, the text on the screen differed substantially from the text that would be printed.[9]

The ease of printing produces papers that are at least better looking than their typewritten or (gasp!) handwritten predecessors, yet even here, teachers should urge students to remember the task at hand. Aesthetically pleasing papers are always nice to receive, but some students try to substitute form for content and end up handing in pretty papers that say nothing. Teachers and students should also remember that it is okay to mix media. One of the nice things about the reproducibility of the printed page is that teachers or peers can mark up or comment on a printed page without feeling guilty for the amount of time it will take to type out another copy (though perhaps we are dating ourselves even to list this issue as a concern).

In addition to simple printing, however, most word processors have other kinds of "publishing" tools that might prove helpful in a composition course. Even with a bare-bones word processor, the relatively mechanical concerns such as page width, margin size, spacing, tabs, and alignment can be productively discussed in class, either in their own right, or as a springboard for a discussion about the physical characteristics and expectations of a printed document.

Most full-featured word processors will also offer basic design options such as tables, graphs, images, and equations. The majority of introductory composition courses will not spend much time on these design options, but a lesson concerning the

---

[9] This scenario now characterizes the difference between popular Web page editors. Some editors are script or code based, which means the author writes the page from the script. The resulting page looks nothing like the page of script which is initially typed in. More and more Web page editors are becoming WYSIWIG applications, however, and work almost exactly like a word-processor. In fact, many recent word-processors can double as Web page editors.

relationship of text and images in terms of reinforced content or visual space could be very useful.

Full-featured programs may also include other kinds of publishing options, such as borders, templates for the production of small brochures or fliers, even templates for business cards or birthday cards. Though a technical writing course may be the more appropriate space for a lesson about desktop publishing as such, a certain amount of this could work very productively in a basic composition course. If nothing else, many students feel a sense of accomplishment after producing something like a small magazine or newspaper, and if that kind of project works into the main goals of the course, then the advanced publishing tools of full-featured word processors can be a valuable asset.[10]

As teachers consider all of the different options word processors offer, they should keep the principle of Simplicity in mind. We have discussed only a few of the many features modern word processors contain, and almost all of them could be integrated into a composition course. However, many of these features, such as Macros, are relatively difficult to use and may require class time to explain. Teachers should remember to keep computer activities fairly simple and easy to complete, so unless one of these fancier tools seems particularly suited for an assignment, we recommend choosing the path of least resistance. For example, if a teacher were designing a lesson

---

[10] Certainly, even the most full-featured word processor is no substitute for a full-featured publishing program, such as Microsoft Publisher or Adobe PageMaker. If the focus of the course is centered on desktop publishing, teachers should look into the availability of one of these publishing programs. If such software is not available, however, a full-feature word processor will at least provide some publishing capabilities.

about arranging the physical space of a page of text, the simplest method to accomplish that goal might be to have students adjust margins, page width, or perhaps even make columns in the word processor. Certainly, these tasks are simpler than trying to publish a brochure using the more advanced features of the full-featured word processor.

Word-Processing in a Local Area Network

The existence of a Local Area Network (LAN) greatly enhances some aspects of the word processor, particularly its usefulness as a collaborative tool. A LAN is a small internal network that links a number of computers together through a central server; that is, a separate computer that controls the connections of all the networked machines, stores centralized information, and manages information distribution. Most computer labs have some sort of networking capabilities (for Macintosh labs, this can be accomplished through AppleTalk; Windows-based labs can use a wide variety of Networking programs, but the word Ethernet has become a common reference for a LAN). Note that a connection to a LAN is different than a connection to the Internet. Each connection is independent, and normally does not require the other to operate. One similarity, however, is that both Local Area Networks and Internet connections usually require some form of user password. If your program has a LAN, students and teachers will probably need passwords in order to use the network. Sometimes, this can get confusing if students or teachers also have an e-mail password, because users sometimes forget which password to use. We recommend writing down passwords in a safe place.

The primary benefit of a LAN to stand-alone word processing derives from the ability to create and use common folders on the network (folders stored on the server and accessible from any machine hooked up to the LAN). In such an environment, every student in class is able to save files to a central network folder, or sometimes, to several folders with different characteristics. In general, any networked folder has two important characteristics or "permissions": read and write. These permissions determine who can do what to the folder, and also determine the manner in which the folder might be useful for the composition course.

There are four possible combinations of these two permissions, but a folder that students can neither read from nor write to is effectively locked, so will be of no value whatsoever. If a user has Read-only permission to a shared network folder, he or she can get documents out of the folder, but cannot put anything into it. Conversely, if a student has Write-only permissions, then he or she can put things into the folder, but cannot see the contents of the folder, or retrieve any documents out of it. Students would need both read and write permissions in order to have full access to the network folder; this would provide them with the ability to retrieve things from the folder and also save things to the folder. Figure 4-1 represents a typical classroom LAN, with the arrows representing the direction of information flow between the network server folders and student machines.

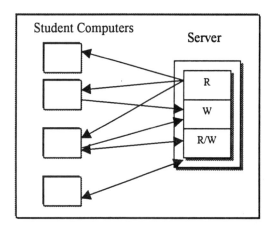

Figure 4-1: LAN Folder Permissions

Each of these permission sets can be useful in terms of running a composition course. In a Read-only networked folder, teachers could place central informative documents, such as course syllabi or assignment schedules, or readings for a particular lesson. The value of this kind of folder is that students can all get documents out of it, but they cannot delete those documents from the server, nor modify the documents, nor add documents. One kind of lesson that might use this kind of folder would be a revision or work sheet type exercise. The teacher would put the text to be revised or the work sheet to be completed in the Read-only network folder. Students would log into the network, download the document (copy it from the server to a local computer or floppy disk), then complete the assignment.

A Write-only folder could be a place for students to turn in documents. This kind of folder is like a drop box or strong box -- students can put things into the folder, but they can neither see nor retrieve any of its contents. Note that depending on the kind of network involved, students might be able to save OVER an existing document if they were sneaky (by saving a new file into the folder with the same file name as an older document, effectively replacing the older document with the newer), so the Write-only folder is really of limited value to the composition course.

A folder set with both read and write permissions for students can be a very useful place for general information distribution, or perhaps peer review exercises. Students can both SAVE to and OPEN from the folder, so it functions as a central storage area. This kind of folder is ideal for collaborative exercises, as students can easily share documents. Further, this folder facilitates peer review and revision exercises. Students save drafts of their papers in the shared network folder, and can easily download fellow students' papers for review or critique. Teachers should remember, however, that this permission set is a double-edged sword: students can delete others' assignments (accidentally or otherwise) as easily as they can save a document to the folder. This kind of situation rarely happens, but teachers need to be aware of the possibility and always urge students to share a copy of their work (rather than the original version).

Depending upon the kind of LAN available, teachers can use local network folders as a "virtual classroom" setting. For example, let us assume that a class that meets regularly in a computer lab has access to all three kinds of folders described above (Read-only, Write-only, read and write). The teacher might compose the daily activity for the class in a word-processing document, and might save that document in the Read-only network folder and give the file a title such as "Assignment 1." When the students get to class, they log in to the network, open the Read-only network folder, and find the file called "Assignment 1." They open this file in a word processor and read through the directions, which might include accessing other files from the Read-only folder, such as a quiz or worksheet. Alternately, the instructions on this "Assignment 1" might ask students to save the draft of their first paper to the read and write folder, and engage in a peer response activity. Of course, the assignment might simply ask students to open a new blank window and free-write about recent political scandals for five minutes, or even to get into groups and discuss the essay they read for homework.

This "virtual classroom" use of a word processor and a LAN can be a very effective method to integrate technology into the composition course. In the scenario described above, the entire class activities could be scheduled and textually explained before the beginning of class, and students might have a relative degree of autonomy in terms of the amount of time spent on each portion of the assignment. Further, the teacher is freed to give students individual attention and help. Some detractors of technology have claimed that technology takes away from the personal contact teachers have with students in class. We have found the opposite to be true. Technology does not alienate class members but can actually increase the amount of time and individual attention we can give to students.

One of the most exciting possibilities a LAN offers is the chance of inter-class activities. If two or more composition courses use the same LAN, they may be able to share documents between classes. This creates inter-class collaborative opportunities that teachers can utilize in a variety of ways. On a practical level, this inter-class collaboration could usefully occur in the setting of an interview assignment. Instead of or in addition to interviewing students in class, the LAN allows students to interview students from other classes. The same idea brings peer response activities to a different level as well, with the possibility of a truly "blind" review by a student who knows neither the author of the paper, nor necessarily the context of the assignment. Such "blind" reviews are not without problems, but they can be useful in presenting unbiased readings of a paper. More creative teachers might try experimenting with other kinds of inter-class activities, such as large group collaborative projects that involve students from multiple sections, or organized peer study groups with access to notes or sample tests in a central network folder.

This chapter has outlined broadly some of the ways in which the word processor can be used in the composition course. We have certainly not included all the possible uses of the word processor, nor even mentioned some of the tools many newer word processors offer. Our intent here is not to supply an exhaustive list, but rather to present some of the different methodologies whereby the word processor can be integrated into the composition classroom. Teachers should always remember to keep assignments simple, and to be as consistent as possible in the computer lab. Perhaps more importantly, teachers should remember to have a "plan B" just in case something goes horribly wrong, and the computers do not function at all. Notwithstanding this unfortunate possibility, the word processor, whether used as an occasional supplement to classroom activities or as an integral component of the course itself, can enhance the classroom experience if used wisely.

Chapter 5

E-mail Basics

E-mail lies at the heart of the Internet, and is probably the most frequently used aspect of electronic communication. Put simply, e-mail transfers text documents from an account on one computer to a specific account on another. In addition, users can "attach" other files to their e-mail. These "attachments" ride along with the e-mail as it is transferred to the destination computer, and can then be downloaded and opened normally.

In this chapter, we will discuss the basic elements of e-mail, including:

- Getting an account
- Choosing a reader (telnet *vs.* client-side applications)
- Composing and sending messages
- Reading messages
- Replying to/ forwarding a message
- Creating and using an address book
- Creating and using class or student e-mail folders
- Newsgroups and mailing lists

Getting an Account

The first thing everyone will need is an e-mail account. Literally, this reserves for the user a certain amount of space on a central computer (called a server). This is the users' mail account, for which they will have a username and a password.

In most cases, the institution will provide e-mail accounts for faculty and students and issue usernames and initial passwords for these accounts. If the institution does not provide e-mail accounts, there are a number of other ways students and teachers can get them. Hotmail <http://www.hotmail.com>, hosted by Microsoft, and several other

Internet companies such as Netscape and Yahoo offer free Web-based e-mail accounts (or did at the time this text was written). Other commercial services, such as America Online and Prodigy, offer e-mail accounts to their paying customers.

Password Tips

Often, users will be able to change their e-mail passwords and even their usernames. In terms of ease and security, we recommend that user passwords be from six to ten characters in length, and should use a combination of letters and numbers.[11] "Secret" is a horrible password. "!t5fry88s" is an excellent password (or was until published herein). Users should always avoid words that can be found in a dictionary. Please note that usernames and passwords are often case-sensitive; this means that capitalization matters. If a student cannot log in to her e-mail account, check to see if the CAPS LOCK button (on the keyboard) is on; if so, turn it off. To avoid this sort of problem, use only ALL CAPS or all lower case characters in the password. Note that when a user enters the password, the characters usually will not appear on the screen. We strongly recommend that users write (on paper) their usernames and passwords and keep that document in a safe location; instructors normally cannot help students who have misplaced their passwords. Students could also be encouraged to write their passwords in code on their course folder, so 807@pearl might be coded "grandma's old address"--or a short phrase sufficient to jog the user's memory.

---

[11] Some security experts advise that passwords be at least 8 characters in length, and include non-standard symbols, such as @ or *.

Choosing a Mail Reader

There are two general kinds of programs that allow users to read and send e-mail: server-side applications and client-side applications. Instructors need to know which are offered by their institutions, and how each works in terms of class activities. As with word processors, each of these application types has advantages and disadvantages.

The Client-Side Mail Reader

When users get mail accounts, those accounts actually reside on servers, which are large central computers that constantly talk to other computers over the Internet. A client-side application is a program that resides locally (on the actual computer being used); several examples of client-side mail applications include Eudora, Netscape Mail, Microsoft Inbox or Outlook Express, and Pegasus. Figure 5-1 displays a typical client-side mail application window (specifically, the mail reader associated with Netscape Communicator 4.5). The first time users run this kind of application they will have to configure the preferences of the program so that the application will know which mail account it should be reading (see figure 5-2). Essentially, the client-side application "calls" the server on which the user's e-mail account resides, checks to see if there is any mail in that account, and if there is, transfers those messages from the server computer to the local computer where the user can read the mail. This kind of application will always have a "get mail" or "check mail" button, as the program must "call" the user's mail account server for new e-mail messages. Figure 5-3 lists typical functions of most client-side e-mail applications.

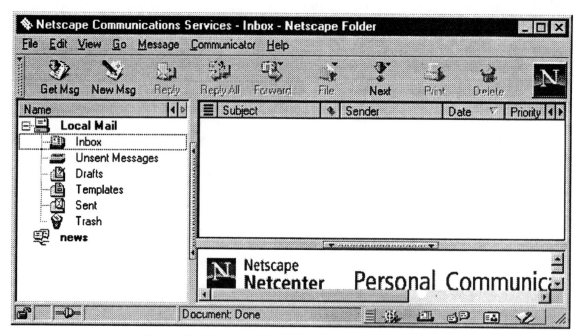

Figure 5-1: Netscape Messenger Mailbox Screen Shot

Regardless of the specific client-side program the class uses to read e-mail, there are four or five settings all users will have to configure:

1. **Incoming Mail Server** – This setting tells the program which machine to call to find the specific e-mail account. Typically, this setting will consist of a computer domain name (computer.myschool.edu), or an IP address (127.0.0.1).

2. **Outgoing Mail Server** – This setting tells the program which machine handles outgoing mail. Typically, this setting is identical to the incoming mail server.

3. **POP/ IMAP user account name** – This setting tells the program which account (username) it should try to access when it "calls" the computer listed above. Users should fill in their usernames here (usually a number/letter combination assigned by the mail provider).

4. **Identity** – This setting will include the user's real name, as well as an optional reply-to address. This latter setting should be filled only if the user wants incoming e-mail going to an account different from the one listed in 1, 2, and 3 above.

> 5. **(Mail Server download option)** – The last setting users should at least check is the download option. When the program gets mail from the server, it can do one of two things: leave a copy of that mail on the server, or simply download the mail to the local machine. If users download the mail to the machine, then the mail will be saved locally (on the local machine itself), but deleted from the server. If the download leaves a copy of the mail on the server, then the messages will be saved in both computers, the local machine and the server. The advantage to leaving mail on the server is that users can access it from any machine. The disadvantage is that users have to manually empty the mail server account (via a server-side application like telnet and pine), or the allotted disk space will quickly fill up. When the allotted mail space is full, new messages will not be received.

Figure 5-2: Common Client-Side E-mail Settings

Using client-side e-mail applications (although these general procedures apply to the most common e-mail programs, many particular client-side e-mail applications will have unique configurations; be sure to read the HELP menu to learn how any specific application operates):

To get mail	Click on "GET MAIL" or "CHECK MAIL" (button usually located in top left hand corner, or in the FILE menu).
To read mail	Open the "inbox" or "in" folder, and click (or double-click) on the desired message. The message text should be displayed.
To compose new mail	Click on the "NEW MAIL" or "NEW MESSAGE" button or menu. A pop-up window will open. - Fill in the TO field with the e-mail address of the recipient. - Fill in the CC field only if you want to carbon copy the message to a third party. - Fill in the subject line with a short descriptive word or phrase concerning the subject of your message. Write or PASTE your message in the content area. When you are finished, SEND.

To reply to a message	Select the message to which you want to reply, and then click on "REPLY," "RE:MAIL" or "REPLY TO SENDER." A pop-up window will appear with the address line already filled out; some programs also include the text of the original message in the content area of the document. Write your reply in the text area, and click SEND when you are finished.
To send an attachment	<ul><li>First, open a NEW mail message, or REPLY to an existing message. Type your message in the text field.</li><li>Next, find the "ATTACHMENT" button or file option, and click or select it.</li><li>You should see a standard "OPEN FILE" dialogue screen – select the file on your computer normally. Click OK when you have selected the correct document.</li><li>Finally, click SEND. The attachment will be sent with your message.</li></ul>
To read an attachment	To view an attachment, you can usually do one of two things:<ul><li>Some attachments are displayed IN-LINE. This means that the attachment is displayed normally with the rest of the e-mail message.</li><li>You can save the attachment to disk, and open it up with the appropriate program. To do this, click in the attachment link if one is given in the body of the message or look in the "attachments" section of the message. Or, right click on the attachment icon and receive a "SAVE AS" option.</li></ul>
To create an address book	An address book is a collection of e-mail addresses that the user has saved in a special file. Typically, all address books will share the following features:<ul><li>Store e-mail addresses.</li><li>Organize e-mail addresses into one or more user-defined lists.</li><li>Send mail to individuals, lists, or everyone in the book.</li></ul>Unfortunately, the location and use of the address book varies greatly from program to program; look in your HELP file for further instructions.

Figure 5-3: Common Client-Side E-mail Procedures

Server-Side E-mail Applications

A server-side application is one that runs remotely from the server instead of from the hard drive of the user's machine. One advantage to the server-side application is that users are directly connected to their e-mail account; they do not have to "download" messages in order to read them. There are two general kinds of server-side applications: the telnet application and the Web-based application.

Telnet

Telnet is an older technology, and typically operates through a Unix shell. This means that when users log in to the telnet program, they will see a screen that looks a lot like a DOS screen instead of a Windows-based environment. Figure 5-4 displays a typical PINE session, which is a popular Unix-based e-mail program. One advantage to the telnet application is its small size -- many telnet programs can fit onto a floppy disk. Older systems or systems on which space is a premium may opt for a telnet program for this reason. Another advantage of the telnet application is that there is nothing to configure; all the user settings are automatically entered when the user logs into his or her account. One big disadvantage to the telnet application is that it uses Unix-type commands, which disallow many features we have learned to rely on, such as COPY and PASTE and use of a mouse for navigation. Additionally, Unix is not very intuitive and thus takes time to learn. A second disadvantage to the telnet application concerns attachments, which can be difficult to send or read through a telnet application. For more information about some of the common functions of Unix and PINE, which is the most popular telnet mail application, visit the Unix Web page at < http://www.washington.edu/pine/>.

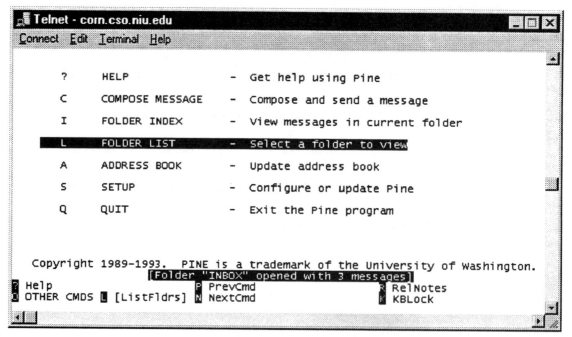

Figure 5-4: Telnet (PINE) E-mail Screen Shot

Web-Based E-mail Programs

Web-based server-side applications seem to be the wave of the future. Using a Web-based server-side mail application (such as <http://www.hotmail.com>), users combine the advantages of a Web-style interface with the immediacy of a server-side application. One huge advantage of Web-based applications is accessibility; users can log into their e-mail accounts from any computer in the world. One potential disadvantage to Web-based e-mail programs concerns access speed: if connections are slow or the Web server on which the user's mail is stored is very busy, users may experience very slow access speeds.

Other advantages of Web-based e-mail applications derive from the Web interface they employ. Typically, Web-based e-mail applications include features such as spell-check, access to an on-line dictionary or thesaurus, and access to e-mail white pages. Some of these features may depend on the version of Web-browser the user employs.

Newer versions of Web browsers (Netscape 3+, Internet Explorer 4+) should be able to perform all these functions well, but some older Web browsers (including lynx) may have difficulties. Users should still be able to get their mail on older browsers, but some of the special functions may not be available. Figure 5-5 displays some common properties and options for Web-based e-mail applications.

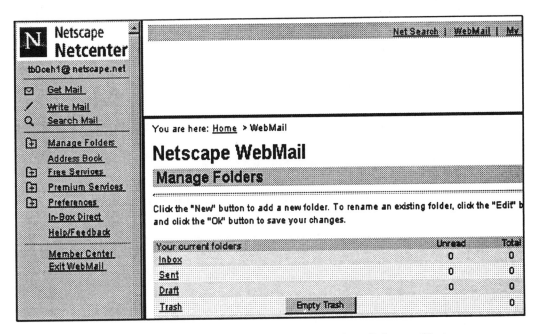

Figure 5-5: Netscape Netcenter Web-Based E-mail Screen Shot

Perhaps the greatest potential advantage offered by Web-based e-mail programs is the possibility of an integrated communication environment. While standard e-mail programs are distinct from other communication applications, such as newsgroups and chat rooms, the Web allows teachers to integrate e-mail with Web-based newsgroups and even chat rooms. This kind of integrated environment creates a full-featured communication suite for students, and allows teachers to create lessons that utilize both asynchronous and synchronous activities.

Using Mail Folders

Regardless of the kind of e-mail application users choose, instructors who use e-mail as a component of their courses should use e-mail folders to help organize class material. If an instructor keeps all her messages in a single folder (such as the 'inbox'), the messages will quickly prove unwieldy and impossible to organize effectively.

In every e-mail application, the user has the ability to create folders. In terms of class activities, the instructor should create folders according to one of two models:

1. Create a new folder for every class activity or assignment. When students send e-mail assignments, the instructor can move all related mail to that folder, thus keeping documents related to specific assignments together.

2. Create a folder for every student. This method allows the instructor to track the e-mail production of individual students throughout the semester.

Instructors may wish to use both of these systems, depending on the nature of the class and the nature of particular assignments. The point here is to organize documents in a way that makes them easy to use and easy to access.

Newsgroups and Mailing Lists

Two special kinds of e-mail programs are newsgroups and mailing lists. Both of these programs are used to distribute mail to multiple users (such as a class), but each operates in very different ways. Typically, both options may be offered by the institution; contact your technology coordinator to see if your institution offers either service for classes. If your campus does not offer either of these services, you may be able to sign up for one or both of them through an Internet site, such as <http://www.beseen.com>.

Newsgroups

A newsgroup or BBS (Bulletin Board System) is a program that posts e-mail documents at a central location. Users go to that location using either a Web browser or a program designed specifically to read newsgroups; they can read, compose, or reply to messages in the same way that they would using an e-mail application. These messages are usually *threaded*; that is, they are arranged according to common themes. Normally, a new message or post will appear as a primary thread, and replies to that message are list below and to the right. This structure repeats itself, so a reply to a reply would be listed below and to the right of the original reply. Figure 5-6 displays a screen shot of a newsgroup thread as displayed in Netscape Communicator 4.5.

Subject	Sender	Date	Priority		Sta.
Re: Were The Pla...	volker multh...	8/4/99 3:...			New
Re: Sonnet 107 – ...	Nigel Davies	8/4/99 2:...			New
Re: Sonnet 107 -...	Robert Ston...	8/4/99 8:...			New
Re: Sonnet 107 -...	Greg Reyno...	Thu 2:12 ...			New
Re: Sonnet 10...	Robert Ston...	Fri 12:24 ...			New
Re: Sonnet ...	Greg Reyno...	Mon 10:1...			New
Re: Epitaph for a ...	robertgrum...	8/4/99 5:...			New

Figure 5-1: Netscape Messenger Newsgroup Screen Shot

Mailing Lists

A mailing list (sometimes known as a listserv) is another e-mail program that acts as a distribution center. Whereas in a newsgroup, messages are posted in one central location, messages in a mailing list are copied and sent to everyone on the list. Thus, if twenty-five students were all subscribed to a class mailing list, every message sent to that list would be distributed to all twenty-five students. Mailing list messages arrive as normal e-mail. One huge advantage of the mailing list is this automatic distribution. Experience tells us that students are more likely to read messages that come to them, as

Experience tells us that students are more likely to read messages that come to them, as opposed to messages they have to go and get. One drawback to the mailing list is that it can produce an unmanageable number of messages. For example, if the same class of twenty-five each posted one message to the list and responded to two others, every member of the list would receive seventy-five e-mail messages! Reading, let alone answering, seventy-five messages can take a long time, and teachers do not always have that luxury. In general, lists work well for small classes or specific kinds of activities. Larger classes or very active discussions usually operate more effectively in a newsgroup.

Chapter 6

Using E-mail in Class

Though the word-processor affords a superior writing space, e-mail programs comprise the main collaborative tools of the electronic environment. Using e-mail, students can ask the teacher for information or help, conduct interviews, evaluate or respond to papers, even participate in small or large group discussions. Teachers can use e-mail to distribute assignments, take attendance, facilitate in-class discussion, and virtually confer with students. E-mail affords the electronic classroom the potential to expand beyond the normal time and space limits associated with the traditional classroom; these extended elements empower the teacher to rethink a pedagogy whose traditional form is dictated by these kinds of constraints. But perhaps the most important aspect of using e-mail is the simple fact that when students are reading or writing e-mail, they are reading and writing. The more practice students have in these skills the better.

In this chapter, we will discuss some of the basic aspects of using e-mail in class, including:

- Guidelines specifying acceptable and expected use
- E-mail as a writing space
- Asynchronous space of public discourse
    - Classroom discussion supplement
    - Flame-retardant discourse
    - Participants in public discourse
    - External Discussions and critical "lurking"
- Attachments

Guidelines Specifying Acceptable and Expected Use

This chapter suggests a variety of academic uses for e-mail; each use has its own pedagogical objectives that students need to understand if they are to receive maximum benefit from the exercise. Students also need to understand the teacher's expectations for using the electronic resource. Teachers who want students to correspond using e-mail need to establish clear and reasonable guidelines. Following are several guidelines our colleagues provide for their students:

- I will attempt to answer all e-mail within 24 hours on weekdays and 48 hours on weekend. If you e-mail me at 2:00am with questions about our 8:00am exam, I cannot guarantee your will have an answer.

- Do [do not] use e-mail to notify me of class absences.

- Please feel free to e-mail me with questions about course assignments and readings.

- E-mail postings to the newsgroup are informal and spontaneous, though should conform to the rules of netiquette. Do not be concerned with forming your thoughts into complete, grammatically perfect sentences. In other words, substance, not form, is what I'm looking for in newsgroup responses.

Guidelines for each classroom application of e-mail should reflect the instructor's objectives for that aspect of the course. If the e-mail message is to be a formal writing space, form is important. Purpose dictates format.

E-mail as a Writing Space

The most basic way to use e-mail in class is as a very simple writing space, and this fact is often overlooked. E-mail need not be sent to anyone; the writing space works as well for most freewriting and pre-writing exercises as it does for sending a carefully written letter to a senator. Many teachers want students to use the word processor in class to provide a writing space for students, but they also want students to use e-mail for some component of class discussion; as a result, instructors frequently end up teaching both programs. As we mentioned in our discussion of the principle of Simplicity, teaching more than one software package expends class time and may prove wholly unproductive if the computers are unable to run both programs simultaneously. In many situations, the choice between a word processing or e-mail package is unnecessary because the simple writing space provided by e-mail is sufficient for most in-class writing assignments. E-mail has the further advantage of guaranteed legibility, and students can generally send and/or print their work at the end of class.

Further, as e-mail programs integrate new techniques and technologies, users can include increasingly complex elements into their e-mail. Almost all electronic mail programs allow users to CUT, COPY, and PASTE text; therein lies the same host of class activities we discussed in relation to these functions on the word processor. Many recent e-mail programs also allow simple HTML coding to provide users with the ability to choose fonts, use formatting features such as bold, italics, and underlined text, and even embed pictures in their document. Web-based e-mail usually offers these features and more, such as instant access to an on-line dictionary or thesaurus, or the ability to send and view Web pages as if they were normal text. While we are not suggesting that students should write the final drafts in an e-mail program, the vast percentage of class-related writing not intended for formal publication (including things as journals, homework, drafts, outlines, and pre-writing) can take place mainly in the space of an e-mail window. This element of e-mail becomes crucial in a Web-based course. While there are a number of ways to provide writing spaces for students on the Web, the easiest by far is e-mail. It looks and acts like a simple word-processor, is very accessible and easy to use, and is something that students might know how do to anyway.[12] Even courses that use the Web as a primary environment for only part of the semester should consider using e-mail as the primary in-class writing space for the duration of the unit.

Asynchronous Space of Public Discourse

The more obvious function of e-mail is that of communication among individuals. Certainly, teachers should also use oral communication in the electronic classroom, but e-mail does offer a few advantages as a medium of discussion. More specifically, we can distinguish three general uses of e-mail for the composition course: first, e-mail offers a variety of ways to supplement classroom discussion and exercises; second, e-mail emphasizes the role of the student as a writer in public discourse; third, newsgroups and mailing lists offer students the opportunity to read critically "real" public discourses (academic or otherwise), and perhaps even the opportunity to contribute to these discussions.

---

[12] We predict that the percentage of students who are familiar with the basic uses of these technologies will continue to rise each year as more primary and secondary schools use and teach these skills as the technology continues to be integrated into our culture.

E-mail as Classroom Supplement

E-mail can supplement traditional classroom discussions and activities in a number of ways.

First, e-mail offers an ideal way for partners to communicate. If the class is working on peer review exercises, for example, e-mail might provide an excellent way for a pair of students to communicate. The medium of e-mail reaffirms the importance of communicating effectively through written language; such an exercise all but forces students into a meta-discursive role as they write about writing. Teachers who use "interview" exercises or units will also find e-mail a useful tool. The obvious advantage e-mail offers is in providing a written record of the interview itself. Further, e-mail interviews can combine the speed and versatility of the oral interview with the more studied and crafted aspects of the print-based interview. Ideally, this combination results in probing multi-session interviews with carefully crafted answers and considered follow-up questions (see Chapter 12 for a sample interview lesson plan). At worst, e-mail interviews quickly produce a series of *yes* or *no* questions and answers.

Second, in terms of simple class discussion, e-mail offers an advantage over the traditional classroom, as it is eminently archivable, whereas speech acts are normally not. This can be very useful in terms of keeping a record of ideas or conversations and greatly enhances ongoing discussions. Many teachers find that group discussions tend to lose momentum and focus between class periods; students frequently forget the specifics of their discussions. E-mail offers a written solution to this problem. Practically, this could occur through something as simple as the teacher collecting e-mail group journals at the end of the class and re-posting them before the next class. If the class had something like a newsgroup available, such notes could be kept posted to the newsgroup, and therefore be accessible to everyone.

Third, many teachers use e-mail to communicate privately with students, and students with teachers. This has a number of fairly obvious applications, such as explaining or getting help with assignments, or any other class-related communiqué.

Fourth, if the class has a newsgroup available (and teachers should remember that some Web services offer such resources free of charge), teachers can post notes, assignments, explanations, tutorials, or directions for students in a central location. Newsgroups can act as an official class bulletin board, a place where students are expected to regularly check for new or relevant messages from the teacher or other students. A more advanced use of the newsgroup might allow a student or a group of students to conduct an "oral report" in an electronic format by posting their "report" to the newsgroup, and then moderating the electronic discussion that follows (see Chapter 12 for a sample lesson plan using newsgroups for "oral reports"). We have found that such electronic discussions can be significantly more engaged than the kind of discussion (or lack thereof) that normally follows a traditional oral report.

Fifth, if the class has a mailing list available (or can use a utility that performs the same function, such as an address book in an e-mail program or a mass mail link on a Web page) the class can use e-mail to communicate *en masse*. Mailing lists distribute every message to every member of the class, so large group discussions could easily take place over a mailing list, and supplement class-time discussions. Again, one of the primary advantages of using this function of e-mail is the automatic archivability of the messages. A secondary advantage of the mailing list is that students sometimes spend more time thinking through a written post than they would an oral comment in class. Some students will always do the least amount required, and the medium of discussion won't change that, but the electronic medium may offer interested and willing students a chance to express themselves more completely or more comfortably than might be possible in a traditional oral discussion.

"Flame-Retardant" Discourse

As both newsgroups and mailing lists offer spaces of public discourse, teachers need to take special care to assure that the conversations remain focused on class activities and within the parameters of acceptable class discussion. One advantage of the newsgroup or mailing list is the partial anonymity offered by such tools; that is, because their communication is asynchronous and distanced, students often feel less restrained by the kinds of immediate feedback encountered in oral conversation. While this aspect is often advantageous insofar as it can empower students who might feel uncomfortable speaking in class, it can also prove a liability. Left untended, mailing lists and newsgroups can easily stray off track as students begin to discuss materials not relevant to class. Typically this takes the form of students posting messages that have nothing to do with class, or forwarding messages gathered from other sources such as jokes or electronic chain letters. Sadly, it is often the students who are comfortable using computers who contribute to this problem. Students who are familiar with e-mail may be in the habit of forwarding silly e-mail to their friends, and such students may see the class mailing list or newsgroup as a similar forum. Worse, some students may engage in "flaming"--sending aggressive, rude, or offensive mail to other students or the class as a whole.

Teachers need to prevent this kind of negative discourse. The first and easiest preventative measure is to explain clearly at the outset of the semester the role of the newsgroups or mailing lists and the kinds of communication appropriate to the forum. The class should think of their newsgroup or mailing list as an electronic extension of the traditional classroom. Subjects inappropriate in the traditional classroom are likewise inappropriate in the newsgroup or mailing list, and teachers should be prepared to enforce this policy. Students who send distractingly irrelevant material should be reminded of the purpose of the newsgroup or mailing list and asked to refrain from further posts of that nature. Students who send offensive or inappropriate material should be dealt with more firmly; the first such post might require a personal conference with the teacher; the second should certainly result in disciplinary action. If necessary, student e-mail accounts can be frozen or discontinued. Even students with external accounts (through such services as America Online, Hotmail, or Netscape) can be disciplined; all such services require certain "agreements" whose terms almost always include an "acceptable use" policy. A simple letter to the administrator of the service should be enough to have that student's account suspended or revoked.

Teachers should take this matter seriously; it is not unheard of for students to harass other students or teachers through e-mail. If the situation gets bad enough, teachers should consider other forms of disciplinary action (truly offensive or harassing e-mail are normally considered grounds for suspension or expulsion from school and can even be serious enough to merit intervention by civil or criminal courts). While we do not want to scare teachers away from using newsgroups or mailing lists, we feel that it is very important to specify the "ground rules" of this virtual space to avoid confusion later on.

Teachers and students should consider this space of discourse as an extension of the classroom and conduct conversations in the same ways that they might in a traditional classroom setting.

One special scenario that relates to an inappropriate use of a newsgroup or mailing list is "spamming." Spamming is the act of sending mass unrequested mailings. Typically, spamming occurs in one of two contexts: "get rich quick" schemes (including pyramid schemes) and pornography advertisements. If your course newsgroup or mailing list is public (that is, accessible to the general public), then it runs the risk of receiving spam. Many Internet service providers have begun cracking down on this sort of behavior, so it is unlikely that your course newsgroup or mailing list would receive such mail, but it is a possibility. Further, most spammers use false or encrypted e-mail addresses, which can prevent recipients from tracking down the actual source of the mail. This can make it difficult to stop the spammer. If your class has problems with spam, we advise that you talk to your system administrator; he or she might be able to solve the problem by tracing the sender or by making your newsgroup or mailing list private, and not accessible to the public domain.

E-mail as Publication

Whether writing someone across the table or someone half a world away, e-mail reinforces for students the fact that they are writing for a real audience. Though we expect most of the e-mail students write in class will be to each other or their teacher, the audience list is certainly not restricted to this internal audience. As e-mail becomes more and more accepted as a common mode of communication, the possibilities of audience grow apace. While students have always been able to write a number of different kinds of people such as authors, professional writers, editors, professors, politicians or other students, e-mail radically speeds up the process and subsequently alters the kind of role such public discourse can play in the composition classroom.

Traditional mail (sometimes called "snail mail" by technology enthusiasts) works sufficiently but can take a long time, often a week or more for a single exchange of ideas. As a result, in a traditional classroom a teacher might design a unit whose outcome was the creation of a single crafted print document to be sent to such an outside reader. At most, teachers could facilitate the birth of a pen-pal relationship.

E-mail, on the other hand, is sent in seconds, regardless of the recipient's physical location. Such speed alters the nature of such public discourse in class because it allows for actual discussion -- that is, an exchange of ideas between parties. Since physical distance is not an issue, students have the chance to virtually "talk" to anyone who has Internet access and to develop that "talking" into some form of productive discourse (either as interviewer-interviewee, student to expert, student to student, or just human to human). Some teachers might arrange to have their students write an author or contributor to a book (the teacher should be sure to contact the individual first, of course). Some teachers might have students find an interview subject for their papers through e-mail or conduct the interview thereby. Some teachers might find other courses with a similar electronic component and have students collaborate for interviews or other kinds of class work. Many newspapers, both national and local, have on-line components, so students might write editorial pieces and send them in to a real paper for consideration.

Students might even be able to find peers from different cultures and conduct an informal international exchange.

We have mentioned only a few of the huge number of opportunities for students to produce discourse that is "public" whether that public consists only of peers or includes a wider audience base. Even from these few examples, however, it should be clear that e-mail has uses that cross disciplinary, professional, and cultural lines.

Critical "Lurking"

While we have briefly explored some of the ways that students can use e-mail to produce written discourse, we should also emphasize that classes can use e-mail as a forum for students to read written discourse. The Internet hosts a huge number of public newsgroups concerning almost every topic conceivable, from Shakespeare to Fitzgerald, from children's books to Creole cooking, from nursing to fantasy football. Teachers might ask students to join a newsgroup and simply read the exchanges that occur in the group. This passive act of reading discussions without posting anything to the group is called "lurking." While the term may seem negative, lurking is actually encouraged by most newsgroups, as it affords the reader a chance to get a "feel" for a discussion before joining in. In fact, some groups get aggravated by posts by "newbies" who have not lurked for a time; the new user who is unfamiliar with the tenor of the group may introduce a topic for discussion that is inappropriate for the audience or (more likely) that has been hashed to death in previous discussions. While most groups do try to help new users, it is considered rude to post to a group without knowing the rules, protocols, and kinds of discussions that normally occur.

This concept of lurking may prove beneficial to the composition class, as it allows the student the opportunity to examine "real" discourse without the immediate expectation of adding anything to the discussion. Some teachers ask students to lurk on specific newsgroups, and then examine the exchanges from a critical perspective (see Chapter 13 for a sample lesson plan that involves critical "lurking"). Students may be asked to consider the implicit and explicit rules of the discourse community, and to evaluate the efficacy or clarity of specific posts to the group. Many groups offer quite lively debate, so such lurking might provide an excellent supplement to a unit about argumentation or persuasive writing. As with any public discourse, teachers should be careful about the kinds of groups they recommend their students observe. Some groups are very dry, some very specialized, some very slow (some groups may have only a post or two per month), and some very rapid (producing hundreds of posts per week or more). Teachers should spend time themselves lurking on groups, evaluating the kinds of groups and discussions that would prove most productive for the kinds of activities they have planned, before sending students out into the virtual world. One favorite activity is to find a group that discusses popular authors, actors, actresses, or movies. Such groups are normally accessible and prone to producing the kind of discourse that students can understand and engage in without undue difficulty. Lurking on such a group might feed into class discussion effectively and could provide classes with a number of critical or analytical activities.

Of course, after students have lurked in a group for a period of time, teachers might want to encourage students to take the next step and post messages to the group, joining the public discourse they have been observing as an active participant. Students may find that lurking has made them more responsible and informed participants and may be surprised to find that their voices are listened to as any other in the virtual space. This step can be a breakthrough for students who realize that they do have a voice, and that others take them seriously.

E-mail Attachments

A final aspect of e-mail that we would like to discuss concerns attachments. As we briefly discussed in the previous chapter, an attachment is a file that is sent along with a "normal" e-mail message. Attachments are not part of the e-mail message itself but use the e-mail as a vehicle for transportation. Any file can be sent as an attachment, though the size of the attachment should be reasonable; most e-mail accounts have a limited amount of space for receiving e-mail. If the attachment is larger than this limit, the message could "bounce" (be returned to the sender accompanied by an error message) or could cause a user's mail account to experience problems (some accounts may "freeze" when the size limit is exceeded, requiring the user to contact the administrator; some accounts may begin dumping other messages arbitrarily until enough space is freed to accept the incoming message). Typically, users should not send attachments larger than 50K in size, and certainly no more than 100K (there are other ways to transfer very large files, such as FTP).

Though attachments do present some potential difficulties, they also offer a variety of very useful options to the composition teacher. The value of an attachment is that the attached file retains its original format. That is, sending a file as an attachment is equivalent to saving a file to a floppy disk and sending the floppy disk to a recipient through regular mail, except insofar as a disk would take days to arrive and risks damage *en route*, while an attachment takes seconds, regardless of the physical location of the recipient. Students can send papers as attachments to teachers or to other students. Some of the revision and commentary tools offered by newer full-featured word processors become truly useful when students can send drafts back and forth as attachments, because students can perform very interactive peer review activities, and perform them quickly.

Attachments and Viruses

One last note about attachments needs to be made here, and that concerns viruses. Contrary to popular belief, computer viruses cannot be spread through simple text e-mail messages. Users must download and then open an attachment in order for a virus to be spread through e-mail. Unfortunately, viruses can be (and often are) spread through standard word-processing attachments. If a student sends an infected word-processing document as an attachment and the teacher downloads and opens that document, chances are good that the virus has spread to the teacher's machine. The only way to prevent this scenario is for each user to have a good virus protection program (such as Norton or McAfee anti-virus), to run that program on a regular basis (especially on attachments) and to update that program on a regular basis. Many viruses are fairly harmless, but, as the name suggests, are always unwelcome and occasionally catastrophic.

A more obvious example concerns attachments from unknown e-mail sources. Common sense will usually be the best guide here. As a rule, users should not open an attachment from an e-mail whose source is unrecognized. For example, if the subject line of an e-mail message reads "get rich quick" or "earn money at home," we advise users to delete the file immediately. Nothing good will come of such a message even if it does not carry a computer virus. Most importantly, e-mail users should NEVER open an attachment whose name ends in "exe" or "bat," even (or perhaps especially) if they are sent by friends. These are extensions that designate an executable program, and represent the most common way to contract very malicious viruses, because they are actual programs that users download and then run on their machine.

The other common way to contract a virus is by using an infected floppy disk. Sometimes, even putting such a disk into your computer can launch the virus, so users need to be very careful about using foreign disks (such as those from students), and should always scan such disks with a good virus detection program BEFORE opening the disk contents or opening any files contained therein. We realize we are repeating ourselves here, but cannot stress this point enough. Viruses can be very nasty things, and some simple common sense is usually enough to avoid them.

On the other hand, we remind you that reading an e-mail message CANNOT launch a virus, nor can normal e-mail messages perform other magical feats such as send you money or give you luck (good or bad). Any e-mail message that claims otherwise is selling something. If you have any questions about viruses, you should contact your local system administrator or lab supervisor and find out what anti-virus protection programs are installed in your lab.

Chapter 7

World Wide Web Basics

The World Wide Web needs no introduction. Though a relatively new technology, the Web continues to grow exponentially in terms of both readers and authors, and has quickly become a standard component of the electronic environment. The Web's ability to combine text, graphics, sounds, animations, and movies make it an environment with wonderful educational possibilities. Moreover, the interactivity and radical democracy of the Web provide teachers and students unique opportunities to learn and teach in ways that would have been impossible even a few short years ago. A number of classes are now offered completely on-line, available to students from anywhere in the world.

In this chapter, we will explain some of the basics of the World Wide Web, concentrating on the aspects of the Web relevant to pedagogical applications. While we do not intend to provide teachers a comprehensive knowledge of the Web, some understanding of how Web pages function is necessary for teachers to exploit effectively the potential pedagogical uses of this tool.

More specifically, we will discuss three aspects of World Wide Web basics:

- How Web pages work
- Using a Web Browser
- Understanding URL's

How Web Pages Work

We have found two metaphors useful in describing how Web pages work. First, Web pages work like a series of index cards. Each "card" can include text, graphics, more complex items such as movies or animations, or more interactive elements such as checkboxes or text input fields. In addition, each card can be linked to any number of other cards through hyperlinks. Simply put, a hyperlink is like an instantaneous cross-reference. When users click on a hyperlink, they are automatically taken to the destination card. Figure 7-1 shows how links work.

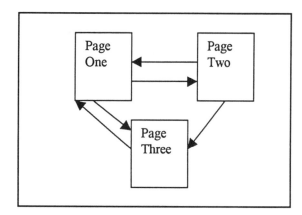

Figure 7-1: Hyperlinks

The second useful metaphor is that Web pages function like little one-act plays. The page that users actually see on their browser is the play. Behind or beneath that play lies the script or source; that is, the programmed element of the page that tells the browser to display "this text" in the middle of the page, "that graphic" on the bottom of the page, or that "this hyperlink" should direct the user to a specific destination. For the most part, users (teachers and students) do not have to worry about the script any more than an average television viewer needs to worry about the script of a commercial or movie. As long as the script works correctly, users can simply enjoy the show.

Figure 7-2 shows the relationship between the script and the resulting Web page. Note that each Web page consists of several files: the HTML code, and each image on the page are separate files.

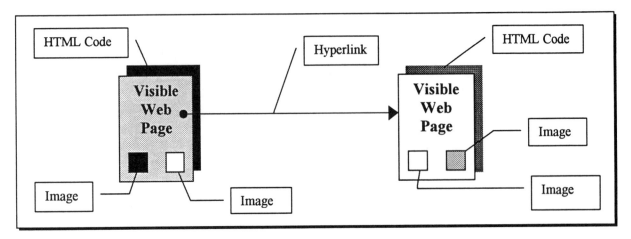

Figure 7-2: Web Page Structures

If we combine these two metaphors, we see that the Web acts as a series of interconnected and cross-referenced one-act plays. Each play can contain a variety of different elements, and pages can be linked together to create larger sustained documents; some Web-sites include many thousands of pages, all linked together in some thematic fashion or simply loosely collected into an eclectic amalgam. There are currently millions of Web pages posted on the Internet, and the vast majority are linked to each other in some way shape or form. Typically, a given Web page will include several links to similar or related Web pages, which will, in turn, provide links to other Web pages. Each Web page consists of several different components, and teachers should at least be familiar with the terminology.

HTML

The script for every Web page is written in a language called HTML; Hypertext Mark-up Language. Comparatively speaking, HTML is a very simple programming language, and there are many sources of information, both printed and electronic, for users who want to learn HTML.[13] Without going too deeply into programming details, there are two elements of HTML that users should recognize. First, HTML script is written in basic no-frills text (ASCII). This means that anyone who has even a bare-bones word processor can write a Web page. As long as the page is saved as an HTML document, it can be opened in a Web browser. Second, HTML scripts can generally be viewed, copied, and manipulated by anyone with a Web browser. In other words, any time users view a page, they can usually view the script for that page to see how something was accomplished, and can COPY and PASTE the script like any other kind of text.

Graphics

Web pages can usually display two kinds of graphics; GIF's (Graphic Interchange Format) and JPG's (Joint Photographic Experts Group). Both of these acronyms refer to file types, in the same way that TXT stands for a text file. GIF's are limited to 256 colors, so tend to be smaller images, such as buttons, lines, or icons. JPG's can display more colors and higher resolution (up to about 16 million colors), so are used for images, such

---

[13] For readers interested in learning HTML, we recommend the following Web pages: NCSA's "A Beginner's Guide to HTML" at <http://www.ncsa.uiuc.edu/General/Internet/WWW/HTMLPrimer.html>; Joe Burns' Web page tutorials at <http://www.htmlgoodies.com/>; and Netscape's "HTML Tag Reference Guide" at <http://developer.netscape.com/docs/manuals/htmlguid/index.htm> for a more advanced and complete guide to using HTML. A plethora of print also exists on the subject, and is widely available.

as photographs or art work. A more recent feature to many Web pages is the animated GIF. Simply put, an animated GIF is literally a series of individual pictures, arranged into frames, and cycled just like normal animation, resulting in a moving picture. Animated GIF's obviously tend to be larger than static images, so most animations tend to be very short or repetitive.

In the same way that HTML script can be viewed and copied from any browser, so can images be viewed and copied by any user. Typically, if a user right-clicks on an image, they are able to save that image to disk. Note that images on Web pages are sometimes original artwork, so copyright protection applies. Some artwork is considered public-domain, and can be freely copied and redistributed.[14] If there is a question about the status of any particular graphic, users should always ask permission to use or save the graphic before downloading.

Several other types of graphics exist on Web pages, but almost all require special programs to view. These special programs are called *plug-ins*, and are usually available for free to download from a Web site. Plug-ins are used to view movies, audio clips, and other multimedia applications.[15] Some of the most common plug-ins include the Real Media Player (to watch movies and hear audio files), Quicktime (to watch movies), Shockwave (to view Shockwave Web applications), and Adobe Acrobat Reader (to read .pdf files).

---

[14] Many sites list and distribute public-domain graphics. We recommend <http://www.free-graphics.com> as a good starting place.

[15] Recent versions of some browsers now include some of the most common plug-ins, such as the ability to watch some kinds of movies, or listen to certain types of audio files.

Interactive Elements

Some Web pages may include interactive elements that invite or require users to check a box, or supply text, such as a name or a search term. These interactive elements are usually *forms*, and do not require any special features to use. Forms can usually perform two kinds of actions: **get** and **post**.

Forms that **get** retrieve designated types of information from a database. An on-line dictionary, for example, would use a form to **get** the definition of a word from a central database. A more familiar example would be a search engine, where users enter their search terms and the engine searches through its database, **gets** the relevant information, and returns it to the user.

Forms that **post** information take whatever data the user supplies and do something with it. For example, a Web site could have a form to report problems. The form might then e-mail (**post**) that information to a technician. For classroom use, a teacher could use a form to have students complete and then e-mail quizzes or tests for grading (see Chapter 13 for an example of an on-line exam that uses a form to **post** answers to the teacher). A more complicated use of a **posted** form might use a CGI (Common Gateway Interface) to place the information in a central database, where it could be used in a variety of ways. For example, some commercial software products include programs that automatically grade the quiz and instantly return the results to the student, as well as provide a running tally of that student's scores. Some Web page creation software packages, such as Microsoft FrontPage, allow users to create interactive forms automatically.

"Java" and Advanced Scripting Languages

One special class of Web page features includes more complex programming elements. These special programming languages are designed to operate within a Web page, so no special plug-ins are required. Java is one specific kind of programming language, but this category would also include other languages and protocols, such as JavaScript, ActiveX, layers, and Cascading Style Sheets. Unfortunately, most of these languages operate only within newer Web browsers (Netscape 3+ and Internet Explorer 4+). Teachers should generally not attempt to work with any of these advanced tools until they are very comfortable with HTML and have some familiarity with programming languages (such as C++ or Visual Basic). [16]

Other Protocols

One of the advantages of HTML is that it is compatible with some older Internet application protocols, such as FTP (file transfer protocol) and gopher (a text-based manner to distribute information over the Internet). This means that a Web browser can read Web pages, but that it can also read information from a gopher server, and download files through FTP. The average user probably doesn't need to know too much about these technologies, but should be aware of the terms and be ready to take advantage of the opportunities.

---

[16] For more information about these programming languages, we recommend the Snap! directory list. The exact link is at <http://home.snap.com/main/channel/item/0,4,-8548,00.html?st.sn.sr.0.8548>, but it might be easier to go to <http://www.snap.com>, and do a search for Java. The above page will be listed as one of the first categories. It provides links to information about Java, Javascript, ActiveX, CGI's, Perl, applets, and more.

Most Web browsers also allow users to access e-mail, newsgroups, and telnet through a Web page hyperlink. Basically, this means that users can click a link on a Web page, and an e-mail screen or telnet session will open automatically for them. The mail and newsgroup link functions can be especially useful in the classroom, as they take much of the potential for human error out of the equation (see Chapter 8 for more information about using Web pages in the classroom). In order for these options to work, however, the computer must have the appropriate application (an e-mail program to read e-mail, a newsgroup program to read newsgroups, a telnet application to open a telnet session) AND the browser must be told which applications to use. Typically, users can specify these settings in the "preference" or "options" menu of the browser.

Using a Web Browser

A Web browser is a program that allows users to look at (but not edit) Web pages. Some Web pages include interactive elements, such as buttons or fields where users can input text, and users can perform these activities through their browser. In order to edit or create Web pages, however, users must use an *editor*, not a browser. A Web page editor is a separate program from a browser (though some full-featured program suites, such as Netscape Communicator, integrate these two programs very closely). This point may seem obvious, but if users have both browser and editor windows open, they may get the two confused, as the screens displayed may look very similar. Users can always determine which program they are in by looking at the toolbar at the top of the screen. If buttons like "HOME," "NEXT/FORWARD," or "PREV/BACK" are displayed, the user is probably in a browser (see figure 7-3).

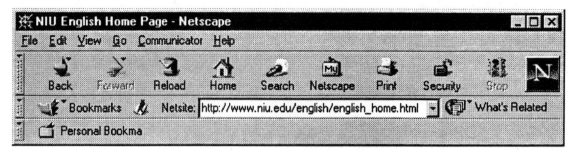

Figure 7-3: Netscape Navigator Window

If buttons like "PASTE," "LINK," or "TABLE" are displayed, the user is probably in an editor (see figure 7-4).

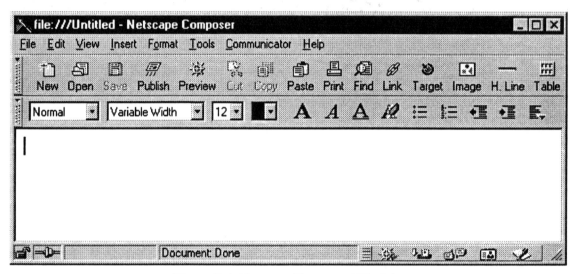

Figure 7-4: Netscape Composer Window

Both of the most popular Web browsers (Netscape Navigator and Microsoft Internet Explorer) share a number of common features with which teachers should be familiar. Some of these features, such as SAVE, PRINT, OPEN, and CLOSE, are common to almost all new windows-based applications, and do not bear additional discussion here. Others are unique to Web browsers, and merit some explanation. We will go over the most common and important of these features.

The "Home" button on the browser toolbar returns users to the pre-specified starting page. Typically, this page is set by default to the home page of the company that produced the browser (such as <www.netscape.com> or <www.microsoft.com>), but users can change this default and specify any "home" they wish. Simply put, the home page is the Web page users see when they open the browser program.

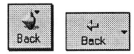

The "Back" or "Prev" button takes users back one page. This order is determined by the path taken by the users, not any internal logic of the page itself. In other words, assume that users have gone from a search engine page to the last page of an electronic version of Alice in Wonderland. If users hits the "Back" or "Prev" button, they will not go to the previous page in Alice in Wonderland, they will go back to the search engine page.

As one might anticipate, the "Forward" or "Next" button does the opposite of the "Back" button. Note that "Forward" or "Next" button can only be used after users have already gone "Back." This button is not used very much, and is more like an "undo" than anything else.

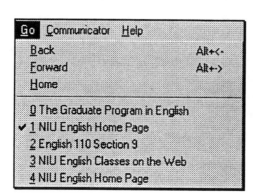
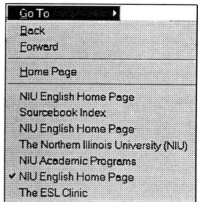

Unlike "Forward" or "Next," "Go" does not rely on a linear sense of direction. Instead, "Go" lists the most recent sites visited, and users can choose whichever site they choose. "Go" is much more consistent with the logic of the Web, as it assumes a more non-linear navigation (dead-ends, false trails, etc.). Sometimes, users will have to use "Go" to back up, because some pages employ "re-direct" pages. A "re-direct" page is just what it sounds like -- a page that simply and instantaneously takes users to another page. The problem with re-direct pages is that they effectively disable the "Back" button, because when users go "Back," the redirect page simply forwards them again. In such cases, "Go" can be used to actually go back (because the user can actually go back two or more pages, not just one).

The "Reload" or "Refresh" button is one of the more interesting features on a browser, as it structurally reminds us of the eminent mutability of a Web page. This button forces the Web page to update itself, assuring the user that the information being accessed is the most current posted. Some explanation here may be required. When users browse a Web page, they are actually downloading a copy of that page, and any graphics attached to it, onto the (local) computer they are using. To return to the index card metaphor, when users look at a Web page, they are receiving a copy of that index card (as opposed to the original, which is kept on the server). This copy is stored on the computer in a file called a cache. The cache keeps this index card in memory, so when the user next goes to that Web page, the computer will automatically use the old copy of the page stored in the cache rather than download the whole page again; this makes browsing frequently accessed pages much faster. Unfortunately, if the page is in the cache, the user may not see the most recent changes to that page. The "Reload" or "Refresh" button forces the browser to download the page again, and thus accesses the most recent version of that page.

Bookmarks are very useful tools, as they provide easy access to valuable Web sites. Some Web pages can be very difficult to locate, and users may not remember the exact path they followed to get to any specific Web page. For example, assume a student was looking for a Web site that provides information about artificial intelligence. The student would probably start with a search engine. By the time the student found the information, he or she might have had to travel through dozens of other sites. Instead of repeating this long process the next time the student wanted to access the site, they could bookmark that site, and go there directly. Bookmarks basically act like a series of personal hyperlinks that each user can specify and save. In fact, bookmarks actually are HTML files, and literally do provide personalized hyperlinks to a user's favorite Web sites. This means, among other things, that a teacher can send students a set of bookmarks for Web pages the class should access.

Typically, users can set bookmarks by clicking on the "Bookmark" or "Favorites" button, and selecting "Add Bookmark." Many browsers also allow users to edit bookmarks in order to rearrange, save, or delete existing locations.

Other Options

Most newer browsers include a variety of other options and settings. Users can choose what Web pages look like (fonts, colors, sizes, etc.), restrict access to certain kinds of Web pages (such as pornography), and customize many other settings. Two special settings we would like to mention here are the options to turn off images and sounds. Though the multimedia aspect of the World Wide Web is one of its more enticing aspects, sounds and images can load very slowly. Some sounds and images are very huge files (sometimes in excess of 200K), and can slow or even stop access to a Web site. By turning sounds and images off, pages will load more quickly. Images or sounds can still be loaded individually if they are turned "off" in the browser (typically, if images are turned off, the user will see a generic picture that indicates the existence of a picture; by clicking on that icon, the picture loads into the Web site). We recommend that sounds do be turned off for classroom navigation of Web pages, as sounds are often distracting (and annoying). The only real liability of turning off images is that many Web pages use images for navigation, such as directional arrows. While these pages can supply text equivalents for these graphics, some do not (though this is considered to be rude by Web designers). Users should just be aware of this possibility, and switch images back on if they are having trouble navigating.

Understanding URL's

URL stands for Uniform Resource Locator, and is the Internet address of any given Web page. Every Web page must have a unique URL. Normally, the URL of a page is displayed near the top of a Web browser, and contains 4 different elements. Figure 7-5 displays the elements of a typical URL.

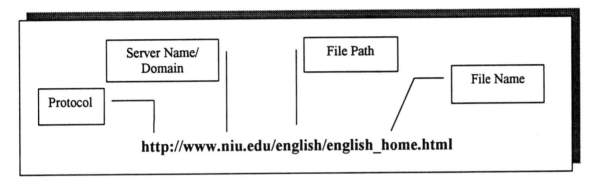

Figure 7-5: Elements of a Uniform Resource Locator

Protocol

The first element in any URL is the Protocol. In the case of Web pages, the protocol will almost always be "http://", which stands for "hypertext transfer protocol." Basically, this tells the browser that it will be loading a Web page. As mentioned earlier, Web browsers can use other protocols to access other kinds of information on the Internet. More specifically, in addition to "http", this protocol element of the URL could also read "gopher" or "ftp". Most modern browsers assume that users are looking for Web pages, so the protocol is optional. If the user simply types <www.abacon.com> into the "location" field, for example, the browser will automatically fill in the "http://" section of the URL.

One final word about protocols: most new Web browsers can also be used to browse documents on a user's computer. Instead of typing in a Web page address, the user might type in something like "c:\". This would direct the Web browser to display the contents of the computers "C" drive. The actual URL would look like this: "file:///c|/".[17] We can add "file" as another protocol that Web browsers can use; Microsoft Windows 98 makes use of this feature of Web browsers by enabling users to perform all navigation on their computer through a Web page-like interface.

Server Name and Domain

The second element to every URL is the server name and domain, which is like the street address of the Web server. Basically, the server domain name (or DNS -- Domain Name System -- identity) tells the browser where it can find the Web page in question, and in theory, reads similar to a street address, from most specific to most general. In the above example, the server domain name consists of three parts: "www," "niu," and "edu." Going in reverse, we see that "edu," the domain of this server, tells us the Web page in question is associated with an educational institution. Other domain types include "com" (a commercial site), "org" (a non-profit organization), "gov" (a governmental site), "net" (a local network), or country codes like "us" (United States), "uk" (England), "jp" (Japan), or "ca" (Canada). Domains can also include state codes like "il" or "wa." The URL of any particular official U.S. state information page is always <http://www.state.xx.us>, where the "xx" is the states two-letter abbreviation. The next part of the server domain name, "niu," specifies which educational institution we'll be

---

[17] For our detail-oriented readers, that vertical line after the "c" is called a pipe. It basically takes the place of a colon in a Web address.

looking at -- in this case, Northern Illinois University. The final part, "www," tells us the specific name of the Web server we'll be accessing: in this case, "www" (slightly redundant given the definition of the "http" protocol, but standard). [18]

File Path

The third element included in a URL is the file path. This element tells the browser where on the server to look for the requested Web page. In the example above, the file path specifies "english," so the Web browser will look on the server for a folder called "english." File paths can include nested folders as well. For example, consider the following URL: <http://www.niu.edu/english/classes/ceh/main.html>. In this example, the file path specifies several layers of folders. First, the browser will look for a folder called "english." Assuming it finds that folder, it will look for a folder called "classes" within the "english" folder; then it will look for "ceh" inside "classes." Finally, the browser will look for a page called "main.html" within the "ceh" folder, and attempt to load that page (note that the above address does not actually exist, and is cited here as an example only).

---

[18] Sometimes, browsers may see a set of numbers, such as 131.156.1.37, as the server domain name, instead of letters. These numbers indicate the IP (Internet Protocol) address of the server. In fact, IP addresses are the actual addresses of the server in question. The kind of domain name we discussed above acts like an alias. Thus, when a user types <http://www.niu.edu>, they are actually accessing a server whose IP address is 131.156.1.37. In fact, both work fine. Users could type either the letter address or the number address, and they will end up at the same place. Conventional wisdom says to use letter addresses for two reasons: first, they are easier to remember, and second, IP addresses refer to specific computers. Sometimes, Web administrators move Web sites to newer computers: the letter address remains the same, but the IP address changes.

File Name

The final element to a URL is the actual file name of the Web page in question. In the example above, the file name of the Web page we are looking for is "english_home.html". Note that most Web pages will end in ".htm" or ".html".

One special exception to this final URL element concerns servers that use "default documents." For example, if a user were to type in <http://www.niu.edu/english/>, one of three things would happen. First, they might get an error that informs them the page they requested couldn't be found. This would happen because the user forgot to enter the file name. Second, the user might go to a default page. In this case, the Web server knows that if users do not enter a file name, the browser should automatically look for a file called "index.html" and go there. This "index.html" file is a normal Web page, so could look like anything at all. Third, the user might receive a list of all the files currently in that folder (the folder called "english" in this case). This is called "directory browsing," and is basically equivalent to looking at an index of the files in a floppy disk. Some servers do not allow directory browsing, but most do.

Thus, if a user does not enter a file name, the browser will probably look for a file called "index.html." If it finds one, that page will be loaded. If it does not, the browser will find out if it can list the index of the folder. If it can, it will. If it can't, then the browser will give the user an error message (probably to the effect that directory browsing is not allowed, or permission denied).

To sum up how URL's work, let's take another look at our sample URL: <http://www.niu.edu/english/english_home.html>. The protocol tells the browser that it should look for a Web page. The domain name tells the browser that it should look for a Web server at an educational institution called NIU. The file path tells the browser to look for a folder called "english" on the Web server. The file name tells the browser which page in the "english" folder it should copy and display for the user.

Note that because URL's are very specific paths to Web pages, the spelling and syntax of the address must be exactly correct. If a URL is wrong by even a letter, it will not work. Punctuation is similarly demanding; users cannot replace a dot (".") with a comma, or a tilda (~) with a dash. For this reason, we recommend that wherever possible, users COPY and PASTE URL's into documents rather than manually type in the URL.

Select Resources Related to Web Pages:

Bebak, Arthur, Smith, Bud E. *Creating Web Pages for Dummies (3rd Ed)*. IDG Books Worldwide, 1998.

Burns, Joe. "The Goodies HTML Banner Primers." HTML Goodies.com, 1998. <http://www.htmlgoodies.com/primers/basics.html> February 1999.

Castro, Elizabeth. *HTML 4 for the World Wide Web: Visual QuickStart Guide*. Nancy Davis, ed. Peachpit Pr, 1998.

"HTML Tag Reference," *DevEdge Online Documentation*. Netscape Communications, 1998. http://developer.netscape.com/docs/manuals/htmlguid/index.htm (February, 1999).

McFedries, Paul. *The Complete Idiot's Guide to Creating an Html 4 Web Page* (3rd Ed.Book and Cdrom). Que Education & Training, 1997.

"NCSA—A Beginner's Guide to HTML Home Page." National Center for Supercomputing Applications, 1998. <http://www.ncsa.uiuc.edu/General/Internet/WWW/HTMLPrimer.html> February 1999.

Powell, Thomas A. *Html: The Complete Reference*. Osborne McGraw-Hill, 1997.

Chapter 8

Search Engines

Search engines provide the best navigational tool on the World Wide Web. In some ways, using a search engine is very simple: users type in keywords, and the search engine returns relevant sites. Because of the vast number of Web pages currently on the Internet, however, searches typically return an unusable amount of data (many searches return over 10,000 "hits"). By understanding how search engines work and a few simple search strategies, teachers and students can make more effective use of these tools, especially when combined with some form of evaluation criteria to help judge the reliability of the information found.

How Search Engines Work

Search engines do not search through pages posted on the World Wide Web. There are literally millions of Web pages currently posted, and it would take even the fastest search engine a very long time to search through them all. Typically, a search engine collects a database of Web page information, and searches through that database when a user types in a keyword. Search engines collect the information for this database in one of two ways. First, most engines allow users to submit new URL's. Thus, when a user has finished creating a new Web site, he or she would go to a search engine page and fill out a little form that puts the information for the new page into that search engine's database. In general, each search engine uses a different database, so users who want their pages to appear in a variety of search engines must submit their Web page information to each one separately. A second way some search engines collect information for their database is by using a little program called a robot (or worm). This robot basically travels through the Web looking for new pages that fit certain criteria. When the robot finds a new page, it automatically sends information from that page back to the database.

The databases that search engines compile can contain different kinds of information about the Web pages. Some databases perform full text searches of the pages in their database (in other words, if the search term is found anywhere in the Web page, the page will be returned as a positive find, or "hit"). Other databases compile only information included in the "head" of the document. All Web pages are divided into two sections: the "head" and the "body." The "body" of the Web page is what produces the actual page that users will see. The "head" of the page contains information like the title and author of the page, other technical information about the page, and keywords. The author of the Web page, not the search engine, supplies these keywords, so their accuracy and relevance are a function of the integrity and knowledge of the author. If a Web page does not include keywords in its "head," the search engine might automatically assign keywords for that document that may or may not be accurate.

Most search engines use this information provided in the "head" of the Web page in their databases. When a user searches for a term, therefore, the engine will search through its database, first looking at page titles, and then looking at keyword descriptions of pages. When the search engine finds all the sites in its database that match the term entered by the user, it returns that information to the user, and usually organizes the results in order of relevance.

The exact method by which search engines determine relevance varies. Typically, a search engine will look through the "head" of the document and count how many times the terms appears, and where it appears. So, for example, if the term appears in the title of the document and the keywords of the page, and is repeated throughout the text of the "body" of the page, the site will probably be given a high relevance. If the term appears in the domain name of the site (<www.*term*.com>), the site will receive an even higher rating. Some engines also consider cross-linking; that is, sites that are commonly referenced by other pages will receive a higher relevance rating, based on the assumption that a commonly accessed page is valuable.

Choosing a Search Engine

Each search engine uses a different database of information, so search results can differ greatly depending on the engine chosen. No one search engine is necessarily better than any other, and users will eventually have to choose through trial and error. Nevertheless, some search engines work in different ways. Yahoo and Snap, for example, work as directory structures. These engines have organized their links into a series of nested categories, and when users search for a given term, they channel the user's search into the categories in which they have categorized that term. For example, if a user searches for "MacBeth," Yahoo will take the user to the following nested folders:

Arts:
   Humanities:
      Literature:
         Genres:
            Drama:
               Playwrights:
                  Shakespeare, William (1564-1616):
                     Works:
                        Macbeth.

A similar search on Snap results in a listing of 6 or 7 categories, including literature, entertainment, education, and dogs. Each of these search engines then lists uncategorized hits, according to the order of relevance discussed above. Other search engines, such as Alta Vista, Excite, and WebCrawler, do not pre-categorize their databases, so hits are based only on the order of relevance. A search for MacBeth on Excite yielded about 10,000 hits, while the same search on Alta Vista yielded just over 5,000, and each "rated" their results differently.

Refining a Search

Search engines also allows users to refine their searches in a number of ways. The most common search refinement technique is through Boolean Operators, such as AND, OR, NOT. These terms refine searches by linking terms together or excluding certain terms from the search. So, for example, if we were searching for MacBeth, and kept seeing a MacBeth marketing agency returned in our hits, we could add a NOT operator and exclude the term "agency." This would exclude any sites that included the term "agency" from the list of hits. Conversely, we could add the operator AND to include the term "Shakespeare" and we would receive only hits that included both the terms MacBeth and Shakespeare. Most search engines include a "refine search" link, where these operators and options are explained in greater detail.

Another aspect of refining search techniques concerns the use of quotation marks. Normally, searches are not capital-sensitive (the engine doesn't read capitalization). If a user uses quotation marks, however, the engine will look for the term(s) *exactly* as specified in the quotation marks. Thus, if we searched for "MacBeth plaY" including the quotation marks, the engine would return only those pages that included the entire phrase "MacBeth plaY" spelled as such. We would not likely find any results.

One final detail about search engine operations: search engines ignore some very common words, such as articles, conjunctions, and versions of the verb "be." If a user searched for "MacBeth" "and" "play," the engine would ignore the conjunction, so would return the same hits as the user would have received for "MacBeth" "play."

Search Techniques

There are three general techniques to performing effective searches on the Web: a domain-name search, a specific content search, and a context search.

Domain-Name Search

The first technique, a domain-name search, isn't really a search technique at all; it's a process of educated guessing. This process entails guessing what the name of the site might be, and simply typing that name as the URL. For example, if a user was looking for Pepsi's Web site, a good educated guess might lead him or her to type <www.pepsi.com>, and chances are excellent that this guess would yield good results. If a user was searching for the home page of the White House, a good educated guess might lead them to type in <www.whitehouse.gov> (remembering that the "gov" domain is reserved for governmental use). A basic understanding of server names and domains is essential for users who try this search technique (see Chapter 7 for more a detailed discussion of URL's and server domain names). This search strategy only works for locating general organizations and businesses or products, and normally does not yield specific information about any given topic.

Specific Content Search

A specific content search is the more obvious search strategy, and involves using a search engine to find a page that relates to a specific topic. The key to a successful content search is specific and targeted search terms. For example, if a student was looking for information about the Orson Welles movie version of MacBeth, they would want to choose terms that would specifically target relevant sites. Instead of simply typing in "Shakespeare" or "MacBeth" (which would produce a large number of vague or irrelevant hits), the student would type in "Shakespeare," "MacBeth," "Orson Welles," and "Movies." This list of terms would direct the search engine to find all the pages that have ANY of the terms listed above (and thus increase the total number of hits). When the engine returns the hits to the user, however, the results would be ranked in order of relevance. The first hits would be those pages that included most or all of the terms specified in the search (and sub-categorized according to the criteria of relevance discussed above), so while the total number of hits might be daunting, the first hits listed are more likely to contain the information sought. In many cases, therefore, it is actually beneficial to list as many search terms as possible that relate to the topic in question.

Despite these strategies, however, specific content searches are not always immediately successful. Some pages don't supply keywords, or choose keywords that do not match users' expectations. Some search engines will insist on giving relevance to sites that seem unrelated to the user's topic. Some topics are simply not covered on the Internet, or are so rare that the one relevant site will be buried under 3000 irrelevant hits. As a general rule, a user should never search through more than the first 50 to 100 hits supplied by a search engine; if the search terms do not yield fairly immediate results, then the user should change or refine the search terms, try a different search engine, or try a context search.

Context Search

The third search strategy is a context search. Using this strategy, users do not look for pages that are directly relevant to their topic, but rather search for pages which might provide links to their topic. This technique is similar to looking through the bibliography of a book only partially relevant to the topic in order to find references to a text which is relevant. Context searches are more economical than specific content searches, because users are relying upon someone else to have done some of the work for them.

There are two basic versions of a context search. First, users can use search engines such as Yahoo or Snap! that pre-categorize topics. Users can browse through this topic listing, and narrow down the search by following the most appropriate path (see Chapter 13 for a sample lesson plan using a context search to help students refine paper topics). For example, a user searching for information about MacBeth on Yahoo might begin by clicking on the "Arts and Humanities" category, and then selecting "humanities," then "literature," then "authors," and then searching only that category for MacBeth. The resulting hits would be derived only from the Web pages categorized into that section of the database.

The second type of context search involves searching for meta-sites; that is, sites that list links to other sites. This kind of search can be accomplished easily by adding terms such as "links," "list," "directory," or "resources" to a content search. For example, if we did a search for "MacBeth," "Shakespeare," "resources," and "links," our results would list sites that contain links to pages about Shakespeare and MacBeth as well as pages directly concerning MacBeth. This simple procedure makes searching much easier because it allows the user to access existing organizational resources on the Web.

We recommend that for most searches, users begin with a content search that includes a variety of keywords. If such a search does not provide immediate results, the user can try to refine their terms, or use the same terms on a different search engine, such as an engine with a directory structure. If these tactics still do not work, the user can add terms such as "resources" or "links" to their keyword list and find a page that might include a link to the information desired.

While blind searching is very easy, effective searching is an acquired skill. The techniques discussed in this chapter should help users browse through the vast amount of information on the Web, but teachers should realize that effective searching is a skill that must be taught. Teachers should not throw students onto the Web blindly and expect them to find anything useful in a timely fashion. While some students may get lucky and find information quickly, most will not, and may become frustrated. Teachers who want students to locate specific information should either take the time to teach searching skills, or provide several good starting points, such as topic-specific resource pages or directory listings. For any topic related to the humanities, we recommend that teachers and students start with the Voice of the Shuttle Web site, written and maintained by Alan Liu at the University of California at Santa Barbara (<http://humanitas.ucsb.edu/>). Liu maintains this massive and annotated meta-resource that contains links to just about everything even remotely dealing with humanities on the Web.

Evaluating Search Results

Once users have successfully found Web pages that seem relevant to the topic, they should then evaluate the reliability of those pages. There are several different criteria that can be used to evaluate an Internet document, and some may apply more or less depending upon the nature of the topic and page in question. The general list of elements to check include:

- Page content and design
- The document URL
- Attribution (date and author)
- Outside references/citations

Page Content and Design

The most obvious place to start an evaluation of any source of information is with the content of the text, which can be evaluated with the same techniques used for printed information. Focus, word choice, editorial correctness, organization, citation method, and tone are components of every text (especially if one or more of those elements seems to be missing) that lend to its impression of credibility. Academic papers posted on the Web will follow the conventions of their respective disciplines for the most part (particularly in this early era of Web document production), as will newspaper articles and public organization documents. Users should pay special attention to clues of bias in the text, as well as the existence of seemingly incongruous material, such as banners or advertisements. This examination of a page's content corresponds to two categories of traditional evaluation criteria used for printed documents: accuracy and objectivity.

A bit trickier than information, the design of a page lends few clues about the reliability of the page. Clearly, design does not translate directly into reliability; anyone with some time and money can produce a great looking page about how Abraham Lincoln was in fact a Martian. Conversely, a scholar with little or no experience with Web design might well post a page that violates every rule of page design but which nevertheless contains valuable information.

The quality of the Web design (whether or not the site is easy to find and navigate, whether it includes a lot of "showy" graphics or if form is subordinated to content, whether the overall look is appealing) nevertheless does sometimes correspond to quality of content. The logic here would be that only departments or institutions particularly interested in a topic would devote the time and resources necessary to create a decent Web site. Users should be very cautious about the weight they give to this criterion. Teachers who are interested in evaluating Web pages *qua* Web pages will spend a great deal of time discussing Web design, and may create lessons that ask students to evaluate the rhetorical strategies involved with the creation of any given Web site, or to compare sites in terms of design and efficacy. Such an exercise is certainly worthwhile, but is separate from evaluating the validity of information in a page as distinct from its presentation (see the Selected Resources section at the end of this chapter for links to pages that discuss aspects of Web site design).

One aspect of design that is important to mention concerns navigation. Web pages found through a search engine or a list of hyperlinks can sometimes link a user to a page in the middle of an integrated Web site (in other words, the link takes the user to a page which, viewed by itself, is out of context). In such cases, users may find a "home" button included somewhere in the document that links the user to the main entry page for the site as a whole.

URL Evaluation

The URL of the page can tell users quite a bit about the reliability of the information. One clue is to look and see if the server domain name has been reserved for the topic in question. For example, if a student was doing research on the White House, a site within the URL <http://www.whitehouse.gov> is probably a fairly reliable place to start looking. As we discussed earlier in this chapter, the "gov" tells us that the server is governmental, so probably had miles of red tape to go through before it went public. Users can assume anything from a "gov" site is fairly reliable information. A site from <http://www.whitehouse.com>, however, should make users suspicious, as they realize that "com" indicates a commercial site.

Most sites have longer URL's that contain information about who and where the information comes from. The file path (see Chapter 9 for more information on URL's and file paths) section of the URL essentially consists of directories and subdirectories, whose names might reveal important information. Take, for example, the following URL: <http://www.niu.edu/english/classes/ceh/main.html>.[19] From this URL, we can conclude that the file in question is contained in a folder devoted to someone's English class at Northern Illinois University. We deduce this information by looking at each element of the URL, paying special attention to any logic inherent in the file structure. Here, the nested folders "english," "classes," and "ceh" are probably a pretty reliable guide to the information source. These names are in fact arbitrary (folders can be named using any legal characters), but Web administrators usually like to keep things as simple and organized as possible.

---

[19] Note that this URL does not exist, and is used here for illustration purposes only.

Backtracking

Users who are unsure of the relationship between a page and the server on which it is posted can "backtrack" through the URL. "Backtracking" is a process of moving up the virtual hierarchy, whereby the user moves up one folder at a time in an attempt to identify a controlling rubric. Take, for example, the same URL: <http://www.niu.edu/english/classes/ceh/main.html>. If the relationship between the file and the server were not obvious, we could erase the last part of the URL ("main.html"), and see what the containing folder tells us. We can keep moving up the hierarchy by erasing one folder at a time and see if we get any more information. So, in the example above, we might try <http://www.niu.edu/english/classes/> to see other classes with Web pages or <http://www.niu.edu/english/> to see what general information we can find about the English department at NIU. Backtracking does not always work, but sometimes it's the only way to explore the relationship between the server and any contained pages. Note that there is no necessary relationship between the URL and the content of a page. In the example above, it could very well turn out that the page we find at <http://www.niu.edu/english/classes/ceh/main.html> has nothing at all to do with NIU, English, or courses. Many servers (such as <http://www.geocities.com> or <http://www.angelfire.com>) are simply public posting areas, and they tell you nothing about the source or value of any information published on that server.[20]

---

[20] Because of the importance of this evaluation criterion, we require our students to include information about the relationship between the server and page in the citation page. More specifically, we a use a combination of the Columbia style citation method (<http://www.columbia.edu/cu/cup/cgos/idx_basic.html>), and the MLA style citation method (<http://www.mla.org/set_stl.htm>) but have students include information about the hosting server after the name of the site (and collected work, if applicable), exactly as traditional MLA citations include information about the publisher after the book title. See our selected bibliography for examples.

Information derived from a document URL corresponds to the traditional print-based evaluation criterion of "authority" insofar as the URL represents the "publisher" of the page, and the relationship (if any) between the publisher and the author of the text.

Attribution and Contacts

Though in some ways an element of Web page design, the existence of proper attribution on a page is very important for evaluation purposes. Typically, pages will include author and publication information at the bottom of the Web page, and usually, the author's name is a mailto hyperlink (when users click on the name, an e-mail window opens that is pre-addressed to that person). One of the best and easiest ways for students to evaluate the content of a page is by e-mailing the author of the page (or Webmaster of the site) and asking where he or she got the information. Most Web authors will reply to such queries.

Pages that list neither author nor date of publication should be viewed with a healthy amount of skepticism, but students can try to "backtrack" the URL a bit to see if the enclosing folder contains this information. Often, only the "entry" page of a Web site will contain the author's name and date of publication, and "backtracking" the URL should take the student to the entry page.

Once students have identified the author of the page (if possible), they should evaluate the author's credentials in relation to the material at hand. Again, if such credentials do not appear listed in the page itself, students may need to "backtrack" the URL to try and gather more information about the author. (In the URL cited above, students may want to find out about the teachers of the course, and what credentials, if any, might lead us to believe they know what they are talking about. If this information is not listed in the page, students could try to "backtrack" to the "class" folder or even the main "english" folder to try and get more information about the authors).

The date of publication on the page can also tell the user a bit about the information supplied. Typically, well-designed pages include at least two dates: the date of original publication and the last time the page was updated. Both of these pieces of information are important when evaluating Internet resources. The "last updated" information can tell the reader how current the page is, though users should also read the text itself carefully for such clues (Web authors frequently forget to update the "last updated" section of their page). The date of publication tells the user how long the page has been up, and can be a useful clue to the reliability of the page. Many pages are extremely transient, and most do not last a year. Pages published a year or more ago, therefore, are probably going to be around for a little bit longer. Note that "backtracking" the URL can be useful here to determine the age of the hosting site. A page on Artificial Intelligence may have a publication date of one week ago (thus conveying an impression of current information), but be part of a site devoted to AI that has been around since 1995 (which, in computer time, is about a century). These elements of attribution correspond to two of the evaluation criteria traditionally used for print documents: authority (to determine the qualifications of the author of the text) and currency (to determine the timely relevance of the information).

Outside References or Citations

Just as print documents often contain links to outside resources in the form of bibliographies and footnotes, good Web pages contain hyperlinks to related resources. Such links confirm that the information included in the page is part of a network of resources, and users should visit at least some of these other sites, as well as related print documents, to compare the quality and accuracy of information. Conversely, users who find the same site being referenced numerous times may wish to visit that site.

One important note about "outside references" should be mentioned here. One of the traditional criteria for evaluating print documents concerns "coverage"; that is, the amount and quality of information included about the topic. While appropriate for evaluating printed information, this criterion is less useful for evaluating Internet resources because of the nature of the medium. Whereas printed texts tend to be somewhat self-enclosed and holistic (we even say that pages are **bound** into a book), hypertext documents are inherently open. By definition, a hypertext is an electronic document that includes direct links to other documents. When posted on a server, these links are active, and alter the nature of the reading experience, which becomes less vertical and more lateral. Indeed, Web pages that attempt to act like printed texts (by attempting to include "deep" coverage of a topic on a single page) are examples of bad hypertext design. When we speak of "coverage," then, we need to take hypertextuality into account. The complete coverage of a topic might span many Web pages, and include many different authors, each providing some small part or step of the whole. This is not to suggest we ignore this criterion when evaluating Web pages; it is to suggest that students need to consider hyperlinks to outside resources as part of the coverage. For example, let us assume that we are reading a page describing recent medical applications of leeches. As we are reading the essay, we notice that the word "leech" is a hyperlink, and when we click on it, we are taken to a separate page (different author, different publisher) that contains detailed biological descriptions of leeches. While the author of the original page did not write this outside resource, he or she was resourceful enough to find and include a link to that detailed information as an integral component of the essay. The immediacy of the hypertext changes the concept of "coverage" because the boundaries between distinct texts are all but gone.

Selected Search Engine and Internet Evaluation Resources

Abilock, Debbie. *Choose the best search engine for your information needs.* The Nueva School, 19 January 1999.
<http://www.nueva.pvt.k12.ca.us/~debbie/library/research/adviceengine.html> February 1999.

Barlow, Linda. *The Spider's Apprentice: Tips on Searching the Web.* Monash Information Services, 10 Nov 1998. <http://www.monash.com/spidap.html> February 1999.

Beck, Susan E. *The Good, The Bad and The Ugly, or, Why It's a Good Idea to Evaluate Web Sources.* New Mexico State University Library, 14 October 1998. <http://lib.nmsu.edu/staff/susabeck/eval.html> February, 1999.

Ciolek, Dr T.Matthew and Goltz, Irena M. *Information Quality WWW Virtual Library: The Internet Guide to Construction of Quality Online Resources.* WWW.CIOLEK.COM: Asia Pacific Research Online, 26 Jan 1999. <http://www.ciolek.com/WWWVL-InfoQuality.html> February 1999.

Cohen, Laura and Jacobson, Trudi. *Evaluating Internet Resources.* University at Albany Libraries, April 1996. <http://www.albany.edu/library/Internet/evaluate.html> February 1999.

Cosgrave, Tony, Engle, Michael, and Ormondroyd, Joan. *How to Critically Analyze Information Sources.* Reference Services Division, Olin*Kroch*Uris Libraries, Cornell University Library, 20 October 1996.
<http://www.library.cornell.edu/okuref/research/skill26.htm> February, 1999.

Grassian, Esther. *Thinking Critically about World Wide Web Resources.* UCLA College Library, October 1998.
<http://www.library.ucla.edu/libraries/college/instruct/Web/critical.htm> February 1999.

Harris, Robert. *Evaluating Internet Research Sources.* Southern California College, 17 November 1997. <http://www.sccu.edu/faculty/R_Harris/evalu8it.htm> February 1999.

Hinchliffe, Lisa Janicke. *Resource Selection and Information Evaluation.* The Graduate School of Library and Information Science at the University of Illinois at Urbana-Champaign, 29 May 1997. <http://alexia.lis.uiuc.edu/~janicke/Evaluate.html> February 1999.

Richmond, Betsy. *Ten C's for Evaluating Internet Resources.* University of Wisconsin-Eau Claire, McIntyre Library: 20 November 1996.
<http://www.uwec.edu/Admin/Library/10cs.html> February 1999.

Stegall, Nancy L. *Using Cybersources*. DeVry Institute of Technology, Online Writing Support Center, 31 August 1998. <http://www.devry-phx.edu/lrnresrc/dowsc/integrty.htm> February, 1999.

Tillman, Hope N. *Evaluating Quality on the Net*. TIAC: The Internet Access Company, Inc., 2 January 1999. <http://www.tiac.net/users/hope/findqual.html> February 1999.

Chapter 9

Integrating Web Instruction

Few would argue that the high profile of the Internet has had no impact on instruction in higher education. The highly-touted Web is viewed as everything from the most versatile educational tool ever introduced to the harbinger of doom. Sorting through the extremes, we will identify some practical and measurable benefits of the virtual domain. This chapter will define and outline various levels of Web integration, offer models for various types of Web inclusion, and provide templates for basic course Web design. More specifically, we will discuss:

- Web Supported Instruction
    - On-line course syllabus
        - Creating an on-line syllabus
        - Reading materials and resource links
    - Virtual Discussion Groups
- Web-Based Instruction
    - Virtual classrooms
    - Daily schedules
    - Daily assignments
- Chat Rooms

Types of Integration

Although there are numerous ways to delineate Web integration, we will identify and discuss two categories of Web-related instruction: (1) Web-supported and (2) Web-based. Web-supported refers to instruction in a course that has a traditional face-to-face meeting schedule but uses the Web to supplement the syllabus. Web-based includes courses that have the primary course materials on-line; there may or may not be actual face-to-face class sessions. The actual difference between Web-supported and Web-based instruction is a matter of degree, and the two provide a sort of sliding scale of Web integration. Typically, Web-supported classes rely on traditional classroom activities, and supplement those activities with Web pages. This supplementation can be as minimal as using Web pages as potential resources that students draw upon for reading or research. A more integrated approach might find the teacher posting their syllabus on the Web, or posting some reading materials. Teachers who use the Web to conduct class activities, for whom the Web page becomes a secondary site of pedagogy, would fall closer to a Web-based style of Web integration. Fully on-line courses represent the furthest degree of Web integration, where Web provides the primary, and perhaps only, teaching environment for the class.

Web-Supported Instruction

The first level of Web supplementation entails classes using Web sites as sources of information. This supplementation is very basic, and requires only that the class have access to the Web. As we explained in Chapter 8, there are a variety of ways for teachers and students to find useful information on the Web, but we recommend that teachers begin this kind of supplementation by giving students reliable Web sites that the teachers have already located, and which the teacher feels presents valid information. For example, if a class were going to begin learning documentation styles, a teacher might ask her students to visit the Columbia style citation guide at <http://www.columbia.edu/cu/cup/cgos/idx_basic.html> or the MLA Web site at <http://www.mla.org/main_stl.htm>. Alternately, perhaps a student is having problems with punctuation. The teacher might have a list of good Web sites that relate to various kinds of punctuation, such as <http://Webster.commnet.edu/HP/pages/darling/grammar/marks.htm>, and point that student to the site for extra help (Appendix D contains a list of such on-line grammar sites). Depending on the situation, the teacher might even offer extra credit for students who take advantage of these on-line resources.

There are literally millions of Web pages currently posted, and chances are very good that regardless of the specific focus or theme of a given course, Web pages can be found to supplement the class. These resources could be the kind of mechanical tools we suggested above (grammar help, citation styles), or they could be newsgroups or mailing lists that focus on a topic relevant to the course. They could be extra readings that relate to or reinforce class readings; most major newspapers now have Web sites, and classes can access these news stories free using the Web. The number of electronic texts posted on the Web grows daily; if the text was published before 1900, chances are pretty good you can find a version on the Web (depending on the relative obscurity of the text). [21] These extra resources could even be commercial sites, such as <http://www.disney.com>, for classes interested in media analysis. The point here is that there are a huge number of resources out there, and they are growing daily. Teachers should take advantage of these resources, and use them to supplement their traditional classroom pedagogy.

---

[21] Again we recommend that teachers and students start at Voice of the Shuttle to find versions of on-line texts < http://humanitas.ucsb.edu/>.

Course Syllabus

A second level of Web integration asks teachers to create a Web page and post their syllabus on-line (Appendix B contains a course Web site template). Instructors can create a syllabus within a Web-editing program, post the document to the Web, and provide a hard copy of the document to introduce students to the course. There are several distinct advantages to an on-line syllabus:

- Students have ready access to the daily assignments and other course materials; they can print any part of the syllabus should they lose their provided handout.

- Students have this access 24 hours a day and can retrieve the information from anywhere.

- Students begin to see the Web page as an additional course authority. Instead of asking the professor, students can (and should be encouraged to) find their answers on the Web page.

- Instructors can make additions and corrections to the syllabus throughout the semester without the inconvenience of reprinted the corrected version. Be certain to announce to students that an amended copy is available.

- Relevant course Web sites can be linked to the page for direct access.

- Materials found only on the Web can be made an integral part of the course.

- Print out the on-line syllabus and use it as a handout at the beginning of the semester. This eliminates the need for two syllabi. Also, many browsers copy the URL (Web address) onto the printed pages so students will have the exact location for the course page.

Course Web pages help nudge students to more self-reliance. Once the information is in place, teachers are able to refer students to the Web page for answers to oft-repeated questions (i.e., "what are the requirements for our next paper? I lost the handout").

A course Web syllabus does not need to be elaborate. As with any educational technology, simplicity is paramount. For example, just because there is an abundance of animated .gifs (graphics files) does not mean that teachers need to over use them by placing multiple, gratuitous images on a page. A simple table or frame with links to the site contents is usually sufficient. Teachers should be certain that the department, course name, number, and section, and semester are clearly visible at the top of the document. The professor's name should also appear prominently.

Pages should be designed to be expandable. If there is a section that has the potential for growth (such as a "links" section), teachers might remove it from the main page and include it as a linked file. Once a course page gets longer than three or four pages, it becomes much more difficult to navigate through. Also, students are likely to print the whole thing looking for one small part, so linking to frequently-requested material is more efficient.

Instructors should regularly add things to the page and remind students to check for updates. When handouts are generated, copies of those files can be placed on the Web. Linking handouts to the course page can save the faculty member from lugging numerous piles of papers around to distribute to those who may have been absent when the handout was initially given. Many teachers choose to make all handouts available only on the Web. Having handouts and other course materials on the Web requires that students retrieve the materials on their own initiative thus transferring responsibility from the instructor to the student.

Creating an On-Line Course Syllabus

Creating an on-line course syllabus can be very easy, even for those users who are not very familiar with the Web. Here is what you'll need to get started:

- Access to a computer with a Web connection;
- A Web editor (such as Netscape Gold or Communicator, FrontPage, or HotDog);
- Access to a Web account (this is like an e-mail account on a central server, but instead of holding e-mail messages, the account allows the owner to post Web pages, and for users to look at those Web pages).

The first two of these items are self-explanatory. Teachers will have to ask their local technology guru about the third. If the local school does not offer Web page accounts, teachers can get free Web space from services like <http://www.geocities.com>, <http://www.angelfire.com>, or <http://www.altavista.com>, or from commercial services such as America On-Line, Compuserve, or a local Internet service provider (ISP).

Once the teacher has found these three prerequisite components, the easiest way to build an on-line syllabus is through imitation. Teachers can use the sample Web site included in Appendix B of this text, or can browse through the Web until they find a syllabus design that they like, and then SAVE that document to a local disk (a floppy disk or a hard drive). Once the document is saved locally, the teacher can open up the document in a Web editor and replace existing information with his or her own. This kind of sharing is not illegal or even discouraged; Web page structures are considered fair game, for the most part, and teachers should feel free to borrow structural elements they like. Note that teachers should not try to use complicated pages (such as any page that uses a special programming code like JAVA or Javascript) unless they know a lot about programming. Teachers who want to look at some sample course sites can search the Web using a search engine, or browse to <http://www.niu.edu/english/classes.html>. Teachers who are feeling more courageous can try to create a "framed" course Web site. A good template and tutorial for this kind of structure can be found at <http://www.engl.niu.edu/NWR/webtut1.html>.

Reading Materials and Resource Links

In addition to handouts, faculty members might put supplemental reading materials on the Web. Some institutions have a library service that stores digitized course materials and makes them available to students through an electronic reserve process. Typically, such sites are password protected so that only students enrolled in the course may access the files. Our reference librarian here at NIU, who has studied copyright issues involving Web materials, contends that the password serves to limit distribution of materials beyond the immediate course; as nearly as she can determine, this constitutes "fair use" for educational purposes. If a campus does not have electronic reserve, the instructor can download materials and store files on a local server for quicker student access. Case studies and court rulings could be easily saved to a disk and linked to the course page for students' perusal.

Links are also a useful part of any course page. A direct connection to subject-specific sites affords students a wider perspective of topics that appear on the course syllabus: teachers can link to information about Maxine Hong Kingston when students are assigned to read "No Name Woman." The teacher might then add another link to information on Chinese culture that provides students with a broader understanding of the significance of reverence of ancestry to the Chinese. When adding links, remember to follow a few simple guidelines:

- Give the name of the site, in addition to the URL, so students know what they are linking to.

- When creating the link, call up the Web site. COPY (Ctrl + C) the actual Web address from the location field in the browser window and PASTE (Ctrl + V) it into the editing box in the Web document (this will not work in Unix). This guarantees that the URL will be typed precisely.

- Check your links frequently! Sites disappear on a daily basis. Try to have alternate sites available in case some links fail.

Virtual Discussion Groups

One of the most compelling reasons to integrate Web instruction is the opportunity it provides for various forms of virtual collaboration. When students are able to communicate outside of class time, they bring a broader perspective to in-class discussion.

One of the simplest ways to connect classmates involves setting up virtual study/discussion groups that are linked to the course Web page. To create virtual groups:

1) Create a Study Group Web page linked from the on-line syllabus. [Figure 9-1]

2) Make each group name a collective mailto. A mailto is a link that pops open an e-mail message form. A collective mailto has multiple e-mail addresses listed and messages are automatically distributed to every member of the group.

3) Provide text that reminds students to "REPLY TO ALL" each time they send mail.

English 103 Section 47
Virtual Study Groups

Spring 1999

<u>Group 1</u>   <u>Group 2</u>   <u>Group 3</u>   <u>Group 4</u>   <u>Group 5</u>

Study Group Objectives

Consider the following questions and issues in your e-mail study groups. Share resources and help guide fellow group members as you work together to compile support for your answers. Remember that a collective report on each issue will be due on Friday of each week of the course.

E-Mail Specifics

Those students using the campus e-mail system will be able to send and receive Web sites through e-mail. Attaching URLs to your messages will assist your group in accessing information pertinent to the issues at hand and can save needless reproduction of materials.

Remember to check REPLY TO ALL recipients when you answer e-mail. This will ensure that your remarks go to all groups' participants. Please report any problems to the instructor. Notice that a copy of all messages will be send to me as well as to group members.

Weekly Discussions

Week one: We discussed in class the importance of AUDIENCE in any writing project. How does consideration of audience impact the personal narrative we are writing for project one? What elements of a narrative must be considered once an audience is targeted?

Figure 9-1: Virtual Study Group Web Page

Group mailto links allow all members of the group to send and receive messages to all group participants. The instructor creates the groups and can keep them constant throughout the semester or shuffle people among groups--depending on the course objectives. To encourage discussion, the teacher might post weekly prompts that groups are to respond to. Virtual groups can also be used for collaborating on a project or class presentation. One person in each group might be assigned to provide a weekly group report to the instructor. Virtual study groups are low maintenance and require students to assume responsibility for collaboration.

Web-Based Instruction

Web-based instruction utilizes many of the same strategies that we discussed in terms using the Web to supplement class work, but integrates the Web as a virtual classroom setting. This integration can function in different ways. Some classes may meet in a traditional classroom and a computer classroom on a regular basis, and use the Web to provide a common electronic environment in the lab. Other classes may use the Web as a virtual classroom, and meet only on-line, with little or no face to face contact. We do not want to suggest that the degree of technology integration coincides in any way to how well a class works. No one with any sense would suggest that a virtual classroom is "better" than a traditional one, or, we humbly submit, *vice versa*. As we've emphasized throughout this text, the Web is a medium, and provides different sorts of options than does a traditional classroom. Just as an artist who uses charcoal produces a different kind of work than does an artist who uses oil paint, and just as the two products must be evaluated according to their own merits, so does the use of various media in the classroom produce different kinds of results that should be evaluated according to their own criteria.

Daily Assignments

Teachers who want to use Web-based instruction should begin with their on-line syllabus. Whereas the on-line syllabus provides a wonderful resource of information in classes that use the Web in a supplemental fashion, in a Web-based course, the syllabus provides a kind of virtual classroom. The easiest way to accomplish this integration is by adding a "daily schedule" link of the main on-line syllabus, and linking specific assignments off that schedule page. Figure 9-2 shows an example of what this schedule page might look like. Note that the text under the "exercises" category are hyperlinks; students simply click on the text and go to the assignment for that particular day. One of the advantages to this kind of design is that assignments are automatically archived; students who need to make up assignments or want more practice on a given lesson can always go back and access that exercise.

Daily Schedule

	Reading	Writing	Exercises
November 2	"Life on the Internet" (CC 341-364)	Friday, November 6: **First Draft:** **"Virtual Living"**	Lab Assignment
November 9	"Virtual Communities" (CC 365-400)	Friday, November 13: **Revised** **Public Essay II**	Lab Assignment
November 16	Conferences		
November 23	Thanksgiving	Monday, November 23: **Revised** **Public Essay III**	Lab Assignment
November 30	**Writing Workshop**		Lab Assignment

Figure 9-2: Daily Assignment Schedule in a Web-based Course Syllabus

In a Web-based course, students should be taught to access this daily assignment schedule as soon as class begins, and look to see if there is an exercise link for that class day. The class the used the schedule presented in Figure 9-2, for example, knew that when they got into the computer lab on Friday November 3, they should automatically click on the "Lab Assignment" link and start reading through the assignment.

The assignment page itself should act as a sort of roadmap for the students, and should contain the following items:

- An introduction to the lesson or exercise;
- Detailed instructions for each exercise the teacher assigns for that class period;
- Detailed instructions about any homework the teacher might assign.

The assignment should follow a standardized structure so students know what to expect, and how to find important pieces of information. Teachers should remember to keep this structure fairly simple; the point of this page is not to demonstrate new Web tricks or flashy pictures, it's to teach a specific lesson.

Figure 9-3 shows an example of a daily assignment from the same class whose schedule we saw in figure 9-2. Note that this assignment includes the elements we suggest; a short introduction to the topic; detailed explanations of the in-class exercises and homework; a standardized structure that uses icons to indicate exercise. This teacher used this same kind of structure throughout the semester so his students always knew how to read their daily assignments. Note also that this teacher uses a variety of tools and media in this assignment: a word-processor, a newsgroup, the World Wide Web, and oral conversation. This class exercise occurred near the end of the semester, which is why the teacher felt comfortable using so many different kinds of tools during the same class period. Assignments closer to the beginning of the semester would use fewer tools to simplify the technological aspect of the exercise. Finally, note that for one of the exercises, the teacher asks his student to arrange themselves into pairs, and for that pair to use two computers for different purposes. This is a wonderful use of technology, because it asks students to collaborate and utilize different features of technology for a single purpose.

The Internet as Pop Culture

Virtual Living
Here are some of the topics which you brought up in class on Monday (with slight editorial modification by yours truly).
- Virtual Community vs. Isolation
- Anonymity on the Internet: Pros and Cons
- The Internet as a Marketplace
- Information in the Age of Technology: Opportunity or Overload?
- Technology: Easy Access and Inclusion vs. Segregation
- Computers: Education vs. Entertainment

Activity 1:
Choose one of the above topics and freewrite for ten minutes on the word processor. When I stop you, print out what you have and save.

Activity 2:
For the Rest of the Class Period, you will be working with a partner. Find a partner, and then sit at adjacent computers. Use one computer to "navigate" the Web, and the other to post to the newsgroup. Make sure that you put both of your names somewhere on your responses.

Traditional Story-telling vs. Hyperfiction
   First of all, read the following traditional short story entitled "Nuko's Revenge" (click on the link provided below). After reading this story, come back and click on the link below marked "Hyperfiction." This will take you to a site that has examples of hyperfiction done by college students. Read through some of the "stories." After doing so, come back here and answer the following questions regarding your experience and post them to the newsgroup (in the subject line type "Hyperfiction").
1. What are the similarities and differences between Traditional Fiction and Hyperfiction?
2. Which do you prefer and why?
3. Is hyperfiction truly progressive or regressive and why?
4. Would you like to try writing hyperfiction.
5. Would other genres, such as poetry and non-fiction work better using hypertext?

Traditional Short Story
Hyperfiction

Activity 3:
Finally, if you still have time, I want you to check out some of the great writing and humanities sites that are available to you through this course's Web page.
1. Click on "links" in the frame on the left-hand side of the screen.
2. Scroll down and click on any of the links and explore the site.
3. Post a "review" of the site to the newsgroup with the site heading in the subject line. Answer such questions as: What is the main purpose of this site? Is this site well-organized and easy to use? How could this site help you to be more successful in this and other classes?
This is a good way to assist your fellow students by giving them tips on resources available to them on the Internet.

Figure 9-3: Sample Web-based Class Assignment

Chat Rooms

Aside from the use of the syllabus as a virtual classroom through daily assignments, teachers can create links a variety of collaboration tools. We have already mentioned using group mailto's as a way to create virtual small group discussions. We have also mentioned that newsgroup and mailing lists can be linked to a course Web site to provide students easy centralized access to these communication tools. Teachers might also use chat rooms to enhance their Web-based course. A chat room is basically an area of synchronous communication, where everyone currently "in" the room can talk to each other at the same time. Figure 9-4 displays an example of a small chat room.

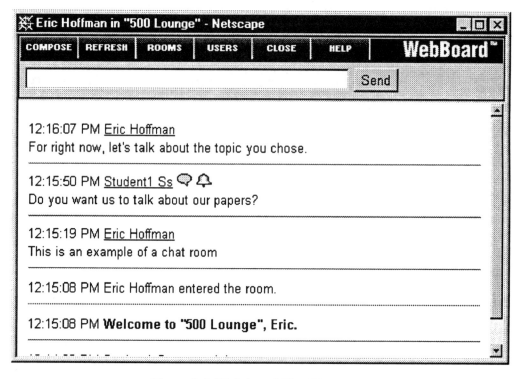

Figure 9-4: Web-based Chat Room

This element of synchronous conversation adds an obvious benefit to the fully on-line course, but also enhances classes that meet face to face in several ways. First, whatever the topic happens to be, students are writing when participating in a chat, and more importantly, others are reacting to their writing. Second, many students feel more comfortable writing in an informal and immediate environment like a chat room, and so become less intimidated by the writing process itself. Finally, because chat rooms are eventually textual, that text can be saved and used for various purposes. For example, a teacher might save a chat room conversation and have his or her students re-read the conversation as preparation for homework, as a way of carrying the momentum of a particular theme to the next class period. Alternately, a teacher might save the conversation, and ask his or her students to use elements of that text as brainstorming material for another exercise.

Chat rooms can also be useful for role-playing exercises. If students adopt pseudonyms instead of their own names, they could experiment with voice or explore a topic from a specific perspective. For example, one teacher in our program asked his students to take the name of their favorite author and discuss what constituted "good writing" from that person's perspective (amusingly, one student chose Dr. Suess, and spent the remainder of the period trying to come up with rhyming couplets). This exercise helped his students explore the voice and style of a specific author, as well as think about the criteria by which writing is judged.

Chat rooms can also be very dangerous to use. If too many students are in the chat room at any one time, conversations can be very confusing and splintered. By the time a student's response to one statement appears on the screen, other students might have already moved to another discussion. This element of multi-linear dialogue can be very interesting and useful, but too many lines of conversations can create chaos. Another danger is that chat rooms can easily digress into random gossip or trite one-liners. The first time a class uses a chat room, students are prone to "play" with the new medium, and we feel that this play is normal and healthy. If the chat never moves beyond the play, however, it usefulness as a pedagogical tool becomes severely impaired. Worse, chat rooms can turn into flame-wars; that is, series of inflammatory remarks that can turn ugly very quickly.

Teachers can minimize these dangers by following the following guidelines:

- Let students play the first time they use the chat room.

- Control name choice. If the exercise does not call for pseudonyms, require students to log in as themselves, or at least as an identifiable version thereof. If the exercise does call for pseudonyms, teachers should assign the names, or provide a list from which students can choose.

- Chat room assignments should be very specific. Teachers should give students specific tasks to accomplish while in the chat room to prevent the conversation from going too far afield.

- Teachers should react to flames immediately and strongly. Inappropriate language in a chat room is no different than inappropriate language in a traditional classroom, as should be handled in a similar fashion.

- Teachers should try to limit chat room participation to 15 speakers. This might require arranging the class into small groups, but will make the chat more coherent.

MOO's, MUD's

In this section, we have discussed chat rooms as if Web-based chat were the only medium of synchronous discussion. In fact, other tools do exist, notably MUD's (Multi-User Dimension) and MOO's (Multi-User, Object Oriented). We have ambivalent reactions to both. On the one hand, MOO's and MUD's offer superior synchronous spaces compared to a chat room, because MOO's allow users to exist in a virtual textual space with furniture. This means that students all enter a MOO "place," and can "see" different things, "walk" different places, and even interact with their virtual environment, in addition to being able to talk with one another (or anyone else who happens to "wander" in). Figure 9-5 shows an example of a MOO.

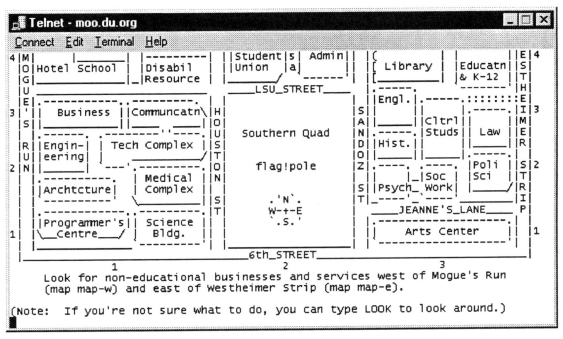

Figure 9-5: Diversity University MOO Entrance

The disadvantage to a MOO or MUD is that neither is very intuitive. In other words, because MOO's and MUD's are text-based virtual realities, users must know the commands to perform any actions at all. These commands are not particularly difficult to perform, but it would take some time to teach them to a typical class, and might be confusing. Our overall advice about these environments is that if a class were going to use a MOO or MUD, they should learn it early in the semester, and use the environment on a regular basis. For classes that use synchronous conversation occasionally or erratically, we do not recommend MOO's and MUD's.

Select Resources Related to Teaching and the World Wide Web

Carvin, Andy. *The EdWeb Home Room @ SunSITE USA.* UNC Metalab, 1998. <http://metalab.unc.edu/edWeb/resource.cntnts.html> February 1999.

Chapman, Ron, et al. *Educator's Internet Yellow Pages.* Upper Saddle River: Prentice Hall Computer Books, 1996.

December, John. *CMC Information Sources.* December Communications, Inc., 23 Dec 1997. <http://www.december.com/cmc/info/> February 1999.

Giagnocavo, Gregory, ed. *Educator's Internet Companion : Classroom Connect's Complete Guide to Educational Resources on the Internet.* Upper Saddle River: Prentice Hall Computer Books, 1996.

Glavac, Marjan M., *The Busy Educator's Guide To The World Wide Web.* NIMA Systems, 1998.

Keenan, Claudine. *An Educator's Guide to the Internet.* Pennsylvania State University, Center for Academic Computing, 3 November 1996. <http://cac.psu.edu/~cgk4/design.html> February, 1999.

McManus, Thomas Fox. *Delivering Instruction on the World Wide Web.* University of Texas at Austin, 10 January 1996. <http://ccwf.cc.utexas.edu/~mcmanus/wbi.html> February 1999.

Roerden, Laura Parker. *Net Lessons : Web-Based Projects for Your Classroom.* Sheryl Avruch (Ed) O'Reilly & Associates, 1997.

Chapter 10

Preparing the Electronic Environment

Adequate preparation is always important for successful pedagogy, but it is absolutely essential for the electronic environment. Teachers need to determine the tools at their disposal, choose those that are most conducive to accomplishing their pedagogical goals, and prepare their electronic environment for classroom use. This chapter will discuss the kinds of preparations teachers need to make before the beginning of the semester and list some of the required elements that teachers and students may need to supply in order for certain kinds of activities to occur.

More specifically, teachers should prepare for the electronic component of their course by following three simple steps:

1. Define Goals,
2. Identify Resources,
3. Match Goals with Resources.

These steps are not unique to the electronic environment; teachers generally follow these steps regardless of their teaching environment, though they may not consciously consider all of them. Most teachers, for example, are familiar with the resources available to them in a traditional teaching environment (blackboard, chalk, books, perhaps a TV and VCR), so do not give overt consideration to this step of preparation. We suggest that one of the benefits of teaching in an electronic environment is an increase in the teachers' awareness of their teaching environment, and therein, perhaps a more productive use even of traditional teaching tools.

Define Goals

The first step in any course, regardless of the medium of delivery, is for the teacher to define the goals of the class. Teaching in an electronic environment does not change this. Though obvious, we mention this step because teachers may become entranced by some of the wonderful tools offered by the electronic environment, and attempt to develop a course around the tools. We firmly oppose this procedure. The primary goals of a composition course should be the driving force behind the creation of the class as a whole as well as any specific class activity.

In practical terms, the general goals of any composition course will probably include an improvement of students' writing and reading abilities, through practice, collaboration, and attention to the writing process. There are many ways to accomplish these goals, and teachers should decide a preliminary macro-organization before proceeding (how many papers students will write, how many tests they will take, and a general sense of the time scheme for the course). The specifics of this scheme should be flexible enough to accommodate any changes the medium of presentation may entail, but a general sense of what the teacher wants to accomplish and when they want to be at a specific point in the process will help the teacher decide which tools to use.

Identify Resources

Once the teacher has defined the goals for the course and prepared a rough outline of how and when those goals are to be achieved, he or she should begin identifying the resources available. In the electronic environment, this step involves identifying three different elements: hardware, software, and support.

Hardware

Hardware refers to physical devices, such as computers and printers. The most obvious and important type of hardware the teacher will need to identify is the kind and number of computers his or her class will be using. Ideally, the class will have one computer for every student, plus one for the teacher, plus a couple extra computers in case one fails in the middle of a class. Certainly teachers need to find out how many computers they do have available, and the general condition of those machines. Lessons designed as individual projects are very different from group projects, and group projects can change significantly depending on the number of people in each group. Machine reliability is an important aspect of this equation; inoperable computers make good doorstops, but not much else. Teachers should talk to the lab manager and ask about the history of the computers they are going to use, their performance track record, and find out about any maintenance or upgrades scheduled for the lab during that semester.

The next most important piece of hardware is a good printer. Teachers should determine who has the ability to print in class, the reliability of the printer, any printing restrictions, and about who supplies paper and toner for the printers. Several other pieces of hardware might be available for classroom use, such as scanners, LCD panels or projectors, CD-ROMS, speakers and sound cards, or ZIP drives. Teachers should ask their lab manager about the kinds of hardware available to them, what each one does, and how to use each. Teachers can use the following checklist to determine the kinds of hardware they might be able to use during the semester:

<u>Hardware Checklist</u>

<u>Computers</u>
    Number of machines   _____
    Kind (Mac, Windows)   _____
    Sound (yes, no)   _____
    CD-ROM (yes, no, speed)   _____
    Internet Connection (yes, no)   _____
    Networked (yes, no)   _____
    Notes:

<u>Printers</u>
    Number   _____
    Paper supplied by:
    Toner Supplied by:
    Printing Restrictions:

Scanner (yes, no)   _____

LCD (yes, no)   _____

Other:

Figure 10-1: Hardware Checklist

<u>Software</u>

Software refers to the programs (applications) that run on computers. In some ways, software is even more important than hardware: the best equipment in the world is useless if it doesn't run the software teachers need to use for class. The most important software teachers need to determine is the kind of Operating System (OS) the computers use. Typically, teachers will find the computers use a version of Microsoft Windows (Windows 95, Windows 98, Windows NT, or Windows 3.1) or Macintosh OS (versions

6, 7, or 8).[22] The operating system determines the kinds of software that can run, as well as the basic functions of the computer. Because each operating system works slightly differently, teachers should know which operating system they will be using, and should become familiar with the basic functions of that OS (how to find, open, close, and print files at the least). Teachers should also ask the lab manager or technical support staff about any security software that the computer might be using, as such software may influence some of the operations of the computer. If teachers have questions about how to use the operating system on the machines, they should be sure to get help well before the beginning of the class; though teachers are not expected to be computer gurus, they need to be comfortable with the environment they plan to use during the class.

After the operating system has been identified, teachers should identify the software that corresponds to the three general categories we discuss in this text: word-processing, e-mail, and Web applications. Teachers should consult the chapters that discuss each of these types of applications for more specific information, but in terms of preparation, teachers need to identify the kinds of applications and features available. Teachers can use the following forms to identify most of their software options (we recommend that teachers ask the lab manager or technical support staff for help completing this checklist):

---

[22] Some labs may run other operating systems, such as LINUX, UNIX, or DOS. Teachers should check with their lab managers to make sure which OS the lab uses.

Software Checklist

Operating System (Windows *x*, Macintosh *x*, other) _____

Word-Processing:
Bare-Bones Word processor: (Notepad, Write, Simpletext, etc.) _____
Included in OS? (yes, no) _____
How to open:

Features/ Notes (spellchecking, grammar, formatting, etc.):

Full-Featured Word processor: (Microsoft Word, Corel Wordperfect, etc.; include version) _____
How to open:

Features:
    Help menu?   Print Preview?   Auto-save?
    Spell-checking?   Grammar Checking?   Thesaurus?
    Tables/charts?   Graphics/Pictures?   Highlight?
    Number of Undo's: Comments?   Footnotes?
    Save as HTML?   Reveal Codes?   Outline?

Other features:

E-Mail:
Main E-mail application: _____
Client-side (Eudora, Netscape Mail, Outlook, AOL)? _____
Server Side (PINE)? _____
Web-Based (Hotmail, Alta Vista, etc.)? _____
Who controls/assigns accounts (central computing agency, department, outside service)?
How to open:

Features:
    Help menu?   Attachments?   Print?
    Account size?   Hot-links?   Spell Check?
    Manage Mail Account Folders?   Send messages as ASCII/HTML?
    Display in-line graphics?   Address Book?

Other features:

Figure 10-2: Software Checklist

Web Applications:
Web Browser (Netscape, Internet Explorer, etc; include version):
_____

How to open:

Features:
    Help menu?   On-line Help?   Graphics?
    Display Frames?   Javascript?   Java?
    Bookmarks?   Secure (SSL)?   Display History?

Plug-ins:

Other features:

Web Editor (Netscape Composer, Microsoft Frontpage, Pagemill, etc.; include version): _____
How to open:

Features:
    WYSIWYG?   Help menu?   On-line Help?
    Templates?   Wizards?   Frames?
    Spell-Check?   Forms?   Publish?

        Other features:

Figure 10-3: Software Checklist (continued

Presentation Software:

Application: (Powerpoint, Presentations, etc.; include version) _____
How to open:

Used with the following equipment (LCD, overhead, Web site, etc.):

Features:
    Help menu?   Templates?   Wizards?
    Web-interface?   Graphics?   Animation?
    Movies?   Sound?   Self-extracting player?

Other features:

Publication Software:

Publishing Application (Microsoft Publisher, Pagemaker, etc.; include version: _____

How to open:

Features:
    Help menu?   Templates?   Wizards?
    Web-interface?

Other features:

Other software:
Name of application (include version number): _____
How to open:

Features:

Figure 10-4: Software Checklist (continued)

Support

The third category of resources teachers should identify includes the kind of technical and pedagogical support teachers can expect for their electronic environment. Typically, the computer lab the teacher uses as a classroom will employ a lab manager and one or more lab attendants. These staff members will be able to offer some technical support, but probably only for general software questions and simple trouble-shooting type situations. More complex software or hardware problems usually require professional assistance, and teachers should understand how problems get reported, and to whom. The following checklist should help teachers determine what to do when problems do arise:

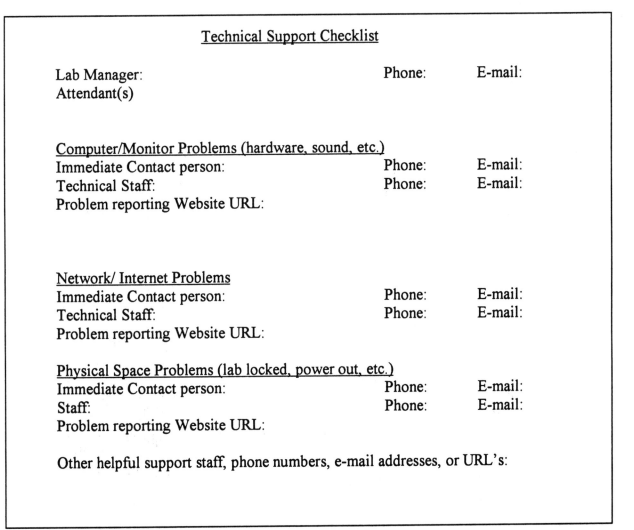

Figure 10-5: Technical Support Checklist

Match Goals with Resources

After teachers have defined the goals for the course and identified the resources available, they should choose the tools most conducive to accomplishing their pedagogical objectives. Paramount in this decision are the principles of Simplicity and Consistency discussed in Chapter 2; that is, teachers need to remember that in order to maximize the pedagogical utility of the electronic environment and minimize the amount of technology time required, they should choose an interface whose use is relatively simple and that the class uses consistently. Given these two principles, the important decision here concerns the macro level of application; that is, the main application or set of applications the class will use in the electronic environment. As we have indicated through the structure of this book, teachers can choose between three main categories of applications: word processors, e-mail applications, and Web applications. Each of these categories has strengths and liabilities, and is appropriate for different kinds of activities.

The word processor may be the most obvious choice of environment, but teachers should not be too hasty making this decision. As we discussed in Chapter 4, the word processor is a superlative tool for final drafts and individual activities, but is relatively limited in terms of collaboration. Courses that focus on the individual production of polished writing may want to use a word processor as the main application. The word processor will also be the most appropriate choice for labs that do not have e-mail or Web capabilities.

Conversely, e-mail applications excel in collaborative activities, but usually lack the kinds of special features offered by many word processors. As we discussed in Chapter 7, an e-mail window can be used as a very simple word processor that is appropriate for most in-class writing assignments, but teachers should be aware of the formatting limits of a text written in an e-mail program. Courses that focus on group activities, collaboration, and process-oriented writing may wish to choose an e-mail application as their main class application.

Web applications combine elements of word-processing and e-mail, and add the double-edged sword of external resources. Teachers that choose a Web program as the main course environment are able to integrate e-mail into class activities, and thus include the kinds of collaborative activities offered through e-mail. Further, teachers can create their own course Web sites, and include both static information (such as syllabi, lecture notes, or sample papers) and interactive exercises (such as CUT and PASTE reading quizzes or interactive grammar tests). Teachers who create course Web sites also have the entirety of the Web at their disposal as external resources, including on-line texts, tutorials, essays, interviews, pictures, advertisements, dictionaries, encyclopedia, and much more. One liability of a Web application as the main class environment is that students can access inappropriate information as easily as they can access appropriate sites. These sites can range from merely irrelevant to truly disruptive, so teachers who choose to use course Web sites need to be aware of this eventuality and decide how to handle such cases, perhaps including a policy statement concerning this behavior in the course syllabus.

Of the three categories of applications discussed here, the Web-based course is the most powerful and versatile. Teachers can create virtual classrooms that are designed to meet the specific needs of their courses, and are able to harness the many positive external resources offered on the World Wide Web. Such an environment can include very interactive elements using e-mail links, and so is appropriate for the course that emphasizes collaboration and group work. At the same time, the Web-based course requires the most initial preparation on the part of the teacher, and is the environment most fraught with peril. We recommend that teachers who choose Web environments for their course specify policies early in the semester, and be prepared to enforce these policies if necessary.

Teachers should also remember that they can change between different main applications during the semester. The principles of Simplicity and Consistency (Chapter 2) recommend that these changes should occur slowly and that teachers should not constantly switch between or introduce new applications, but they are not intended to lock teachers into an application. For example, during the beginning of a course, an e-mail or Web application may be very useful for generating drafts, collecting information, or facilitating collaborative work. Near the middle or end of the semester, however, teachers may want to switch to a word-processing application as students begin working on final polished drafts.

Chapter 11

Entering the Electronic Environment

First impressions are crucial. The initial computer class can be a great opportunity to foster a positive attitude toward technology among students. Instructors can start this conditioning during the first class period by explaining how technology will be an integral component of the course writing experience; students who understand that technology is essential to course objectives are more likely to establish their expectations of the class experience more realistically. Instructors will find that lab sessions designed to encourage interaction and simulate actual course functions in a non-threatening format will be the least frustrating and most useful to students. This chapter outlines procedures for planning before the semester starts in addition to what to do (and how to do it) on the first several lab days.

Before Going to Lab

Following are suggestions for pre-lab planning:

1. Create an on-line syllabus for the course (see Appendix B for a course page template). Use a printed copy as the course syllabus to hand out on day one; when printed from Netscape and many Internet browsers, the pages will have the URL at the top, a great reference that makes it easier for students to find the site. Include instructor's e-mail address on the document.

2. Outline lab information in the syllabus including:

   A. Where and when students will be using lab.

   B. Objectives for electronic components of course.

   C. What to take to lab each time:

      1) How many and what type of disks (Preformatted? Macintosh? Zip? Back-ups?).

      2) Inexpensive disk-protecting case (have a sample to show class).

      3) Texts, portfolio of activities.

      4) Login number and password.

3. Login information (where applicable):

   A. Obtain students' login identification information for both the Local Area Network (where applicable) and e-mail accounts (see Chapters 4 and 5 for more information about LAN's and e-mail accounts). Many universities provide these automatically for classes with a lab component. On the first lab day, give each student a 3x5 index card with login id numbers.

   B. Or, require students to get their own login information.

      1) Provide instructions for where and how to get login ids.

      2) Set deadline by when students must provide instructor with login ids. Be certain deadline is several days before initial computer session to ensure that all students have access on first lab day.

      3) Include this requirement in course syllabus.

      4) Keep a list of all login ids.

4. Arrange for help the first day:

   A. Request assistance of lab attendant who can either provide a lab introduction or assist the instructor with such an introduction.

   B. If lab assistance is unavailable, arrange for a colleague to help in exchange for assistance in his or her first lab session -- the "buddy system."

5. Be well prepared:

   A. Go to lab where class is held; walk through procedures to be introduced to students. (Note: doing a remote login to the lab may produce slightly different prompts; going physically to lab ensures that all procedures will be precisely what students see when they get to class).

   B. Document these steps in writing.

   C. Prepare instructions for students. A brief outline form of steps is most effective.

6. In the class period before first lab, briefly explain what students will be doing in lab and outline objectives.

Day One

Many students are apprehensive about technology, so it is imperative that instructors plan first day activities that provide the basic information students will need to successfully use the lab during out-of-class hours. Teachers should be careful not to attempt too much or students will be overwhelmed. Just how much is too much can be determined by personally doing the assignment step by step and making adjustments, by trial and error, and by seeking the advice of experienced colleagues. Having an extra person available to walk among students and offer direct assistance during the introductory session provides a smoother presentation, because if the speaker does not have to stop and address individual problems, he or she is able to concentrate on the overall process rather than glitches.

<u>Introduction to Lab</u> (conducted by lab assistant or instructor).
1. Lab policies and hours.
2. Basic information on what programs are available.
3. Information about accessing system:
    a. Turning on machines.
    b. Login procedures (where applicable).
    c. A brief overview on entering and exiting basic programs including word processing, e-mail, Internet.
4. Accessing the on-line course syllabus:
    a. Take students to the site and review the course Web site features. Be certain students bookmark the site or record the URL so they can easily find the page outside class. Provide guidelines for what students can expect from the site.
    b. Have students send instructor an e-mail message to be certain their e-mail accounts are functioning.
5. How to open and save a file in word processor.
6. Conduct an informal activity that serves as a review of the introduction.
7. Logging off and shutting down system

Following the introduction to the lab, the class should enter and use the main application environment. Teachers should have a very simple activity planned for this initial class period designed to help students become familiar with the kinds of features they will be using most often during the semester. If the main environment is an e-mail supplemented Web site, for example, teachers will probably want students to enter the Web site and send an introductory e-mail message to themselves or to the class as a whole if the class has something like a newsgroup or mailing list.[23] Teachers should hold office hours in the lab on two set occasions and inform students that those who come will receive individual or small-group reviews of introductory topics.

---

[23] For more information about e-mail, newsgroups, and mailing lists, see Chapters 5 and 6.

Suggestions for First Day Activities

Interactive/Continuous Narrative ("musical computers")

<u>Pedagogical objective</u>: The creative nature of this activity gets students instantly involved in writing a narrative without time to worry about a topic. In addition, they must carefully read the work of others' and quickly contribute to the narrative thread. In the process of moving from machine to machine, students will physically bump into each other, promoting a less structured and more informal environment that encourages interaction (an excellent get acquainted activity!). Remind students to observe rules of courtesy and refrain from typing things that might be offensive to others.

<u>Technology skill(s)</u>: Students practice typing and saving without thinking about these functions as independent skills. Since there are no detailed directions for this activity, students feel the freedom to simply write and move on without the frustration of an overwhelming list of commands to master: they simply type and move on. This exercise familiarizes students with the word-processing feature of whatever application the class is using, whether it is an e-mail window, a word processor as such, or a portion of a Web site.

<u>Process</u>:
[Teachers should provide a brief description (oral or written) of how to OPEN and SAVE a file; be certain to identify where the file should be saved or sent.]

1. Open a new document and save it as "story."*
2. Begin by typing a sentence to serve as the opening of a narrative. This step should take no longer than 2 or 3 minutes.
3. Move to the computer to your right and add a sentence to the opening.
4. Proceed by rows or zones around the lab until [the allotted time is almost up].
5. Conclude the next story you contribute to, then return to the computer where you started.
6. Raise your hand if you would like to share your story with class.

<u>Notes</u>:
*(If the class is using an e-mail composition window, students should click on "new message" and put "story" in the subject line. Instead of, or in addition to, saving the document, they can send a copy to the teacher, themselves, the course newsgroup, or mailing list.)

Completed stories can also be printed and shared with the group at another meeting, or sent through e-mail. If the teacher is concerned about inappropriate contributions, have students write down an alias along with their real name and submit it at the beginning of the activity. Recommend that students select a short and easy-to-type alias. Only the instructor will know the pseudonym so anonymity is preserved. Have students add the selected alias after each sentence they contribute at each workstation.

First-Day Reaction Statement

Pedagogical objective: This exercise provides students an opportunity to express in writing their impressions concerning their initial lab experience. Students must think about, evaluate, and articulate their reactions in written form.

Technology skill(s): Students learn to OPEN, SAVE, and PRINT a document. Since this statement is only a small part of the first-day experience, be careful not to become too ambitious in asking students to practice other word processing skills (as COPY and PASTE, etc.). Again, this exercise can be completed in an e-mail composition screen instead of a word processor.

Process:
[Provide a brief description of how to OPEN, SAVE (SEND) and PRINT a file; be certain to identify where the file should be saved.]
1. OPEN a new document and SAVE it as "statement."*
2. Write two or three paragraphs that detail your experience in this first lab session. You might want to include things like:
   - how you felt about your abilities with computers at the beginning of class
   - how you feel about your abilities now
   - what kinds of problems you had today
   - how the lab might compliment what you already know
   - anything else you feel is important to relate
3. SAVE and PRINT the document.

Notes:
*If the class is using an e-mail composition window, students should click on "NEW MESSAGE" and put "statement" in the subject line. Instead of or in addition to saving the document, they can send a copy to the teacher, themselves, the course newsgroup, or mailing list. In step 3, have students SEND the e-mail rather than print the file.

Teachers should feel free to change the prompts suggested above. Teachers might also want to ban "easy" words from the assignment. Rather than stating that lab was "boring" or "hard," require students to detail their reactions instead of falling back on non-descriptors. The key to success with this assignment is to keep it technologically simple but relevant to the principles of writing stressed in the course.

Day Two

The most important aspect of the second day in lab is for teachers to reinforce the processes introduced in the first (following the principle of Consistency discussed in Chapter 2). Teachers may want to summarize the main points covered in the lab introduction, or ask the lab attendant to do so. More importantly, teachers should again guide students to and through the course Web site or on-line syllabus, and then help students enter the main application. The principle of Consistency is essential for the second lab day; students may be feeling overwhelmed by the technology introduced in the first class, and the second lab day should not introduce any new elements. Rather, teachers should use this second class to bolster the confidence of students by reinforcing their ability to perform the steps required to access the main application of the course.

For example, if the class is going to use an e-mail enhanced Web site as the main class application, then the activities of the first day probably had students write and send a simple introductory e-mail to the teacher or class. The second lab day should not introduce any new elements, so the teacher might ask students to visit the class Web site again and write another e-mail. The subject of this second e-mail can vary, and should probably be tied more directly to a writing objective than was the first assignment, but the process itself (how to open the program, check e-mail, compose a new message, or reply to an existing message) should not change.

Again, teachers may want to arrange for extra help on the second lab day. Extra bodies to help answer technical or operational questions from students always help make the first few lab days more productive.

Suggestions for Second Day Activities

Comparative Summaries

<u>Pedagogical Objective</u>: This activity asks students to summarize a short work (essay, poem, or advertisement). Students then exchange summaries, and carefully read through their partner's summary. Finally, students consider and write about the differences between the summaries, and what such differences imply about the nature of summary.

<u>Technology Skill(s)</u>: This activity reinforces basic writing skills (how to OPEN a new document and SAVE or SEND that document), and can be used easily in either word processing or e-mail applications.

<u>Process</u>:
1. Pick partners (groups of three will also work). [If using e-mail, students should exchange e-mail addresses with other group members].
2. Open a new document and save it as "summary." [If the class is using an e-mail composition window, students should click on "NEW MESSAGE" and put "summary" in the subject line. They should address the mail to their group partners].
3. Take out your reading, and scan through it quickly to familiarize yourself with the main points in the text.
4. Summarize the text. Do not simply list features, but describe the key points of the text in your own words, in order of importance.
5. Save your document. [If the class is using e-mail, have students SEND the text to their partners].
6. Exchange your summary with your partner and read his or her summary. [If the course is using a word processor, students can simply switch computers or print the document and exchange hard copies; if using e-mail, students should just send it to their partners].
7. In a separate document, consider and write down the differences between the summaries, including the points included and the order of importance given to the points.
8. Save your comparative summary document.
9. Print it out and hand it in to me by the end of class.

<u>Notes</u>:

    This exercise requires that students have read a text that they can summarize: use an essay from your textbook, a short text found on the Web, even an advertisement or recent news event. Teachers who wish to expand this exercise into a more group activity can have each group create a collaborative summary, and then exchange group summaries with another group, and repeat step 7. In theory, this step can be repeated until the class as a whole creates one mass comparative summary.

    Alternately, courses with the appropriate tools can have students post their initial summaries to the course newsgroup, mailing list, or shared network folder and conduct step 7 as a large group activity instead of in small groups.

Second Day Reaction Statement

<u>Pedagogical objective</u>: This exercise reinforces meta-cognitive aspects of writing and learning. Students must again think about, evaluate, and articulate their reactions in written form.

<u>Technology skill(s)</u>: Reinforces familiarity with word-processing features of electronic environment (how to OPEN, SAVE/SEND and PRINT a file).

<u>Process</u>:
1. OPEN a new document and SAVE it as "statement2."*
2. Write two or three paragraphs that detail your experience in this second lab session. As you write this text, focus on the differences or similarities of your reactions from the first lab day. You may also want to consider more specifically how you feel about the act of writing in the electronic environment.
3. Save and print the document.

<u>Notes</u>:
*If the class is using an e-mail composition window, students should click on "new message" and put "statement2" in the subject line. Instead of or in addition to saving the document, they can send a copy to the teacher, themselves, the course newsgroup, or mailing list.

As with the first reaction exercise, teachers may wish to consider banning "easy" words from the assignment. Teachers may also want to standardize this kind of exercise into a sort of electronic writing journal that students can save and place into a writing portfolio at the end of the semester.

Chapter 12

Word-Processing Lesson Plan Samples

This chapter outlines some of the specific ways that the word processor can be used in the composition course. We have certainly not included all the possible uses of the word processor, nor even mentioned some of the tools many newer word processors offer. Our intent here is not to supply an exhaustive list, but rather to present some of the different methodologies whereby the word processor can be integrated into the composition classroom. Teachers should always remember to keep assignments simple, and to be as consistent as possible in the computer lab. Perhaps more importantly, teachers should remember the principle of Preparation, and to have a "plan B" just in case something goes horribly wrong, and the computers do not function at all.

One important consideration about using the word processor in class concerns the way the teacher distributes the assignment to the class. If the class is using a networked computer lab with access to a LAN, teachers can distribute assignments using shared network folders (see Chapter 4 for more details). If the lab does not have a LAN, but does have Internet access, teachers may want to consider distributing exercises using e-mail or a Web page interface that allows students to download word-processing files. If the lab has neither a LAN nor an Internet connection, teachers can use an LCD projector or overhead projection panel to display the assignment onto a central screen, where students can all read through and start the assignment. Alternately, teachers might wish to write the exercise on a whiteboard (we are assuming the computer labs do not have chalkboards, as chalk dust is very bad for computers). Whichever presentation style the teacher uses, we strongly recommend that he or she stay with this format for a number of classes (following the principle of Consistency discussed in Chapter 2).

A final note about the format of the exercises that follow: each exercise is divided into five sections. The "Pedagogical Objective" summarizes the writing goals of the exercise, while the "Technology Skill(s)" section summarizes the computer skills students will need to use. The "Process" section contains the exercise itself, and is designed to be used directly, or modified at the teacher's discretion. Teachers will note that the process sections are very detail oriented, listing the different steps students need to follow to complete the assignment. Following the "Process" section, the "Notes" section includes additional information about the exercise for the teacher. The final section, "Plan B," gives non-electronic adaptations of the exercise where possible, in case computers crash or become otherwise unusable.

Many of these exercises use common word processor applications, such as SAVE, SAVE AS, OPEN, CUT, PASTE, and PRINT. Teachers should consider spending some time reviewing these procedures before having the class work on the activtity. We encourage teachers to have students access the HELP menu in order to review these processes, or to copy and hand out the tables we provided in Chapter 3.

Collaborative Word-Processing Stories*

<u>Pedagogical Objective</u>: To introduce students to the electronic environment in general, word processing in particular, and to foster a sense of writing community in small groups.

<u>Technology Skill(s)</u>: Basic word-processing.

<u>Process</u>:
1. Get into small groups of 4 or 5. Every student should be at his or her own computer.
2. Open a new blank document.
3. Write a sentence that introduces a story.
4. When you are done, switch computers with the member of your group sitting to your right, and write the second sentence of that story.
5. Continue this process until you have made two complete loops (that is, until you have written two sentences for each of the stories in your group.
6. As you are now back at your original story, read through and then write a sentence that concludes your story.
7. Save your document. Give it an appropriate title.
8. Taking turns, have every group member read his or her story out loud. As a group, pick one story to read out loud to the rest of the class.

<u>Notes</u>:
    This exercise is a great icebreaker, and should be used near the beginning of the semester. Teachers can expand this exercise by having students perform a revision loop after the initial story has been written. In this variation, the students would be able to change any one sentence in each story however they wanted.

<u>Plan B</u>:
    This exercise can be accomplished using pencil and paper as easily as it can using the computer.

* This exercise is a version of the exercise included under "first day activities" in Chapter 11.

Freewriting Journal

<u>Pedagogical Objective</u>: Students freewrite into a word-processing file saved as a journal. This exercise helps students get comfortable with the electronic writing space, and may be used to explore different features of the program.

<u>Technology skill(s)</u>: Using a word processor.

<u>Process</u>:
1. Open a new blank document in the word processor. Before typing anything, SAVE the file as "*yourlastname* journal."
2. To begin, type in today's date, or use the INSERT DATE command in your word processor (access the help menu if necessary).
3. Freewrite for 10 minutes; that is, type for 10 minutes without pausing to consider what you are writing. You can turn off your monitor if you find yourself distracted by the words you are typing. When you finish, be sure to SAVE your document again.
4. After you are done, read through what you have written, and try to assign a "topic" sentence at the beginning of the journal entry.

<u>Notes</u>:
As students work on their free-writing journals, they can either add to the existing document, separating each entry with the new date and topic sentence, or create separate files for each entry. These journals can also be used for focused freewriting exercises, where the teacher supplies the topic.

Teachers are encouraged to refer back to these files as possible brainstorming sources, as students can easily COPY and PASTE text from the freewriting journal into a rough draft of a paper or another exercise.

<u>Plan B</u>:
Perhaps obviously, this exercise can also be done using pencil and paper.

Spellcheck: Text Manipulation Activity

<u>Pedagogical objective</u>: This activity is low key and encourages students to critically read and evaluate existing text rather than attempt to generate their own selection.

<u>Technology skill(s)</u>: Introduce students to the fundamentals of word processing. Include in the directions the features that students will use most frequently in class. For difficult functions, provide a brief description of how to perform the function or point students to the HELP menu.

<u>Process</u>:
1. Below is a short essay on technology. Quickly (take no more than 5 minutes) read through the text and then perform the requested functions below. Pay special attention to the spell check and proofreading instructions--there are words deliberately misspelled and misused throughout the selection.
2. SAVE the file as "activity1."
3. Single-space the document.
4. Center the title (remember, to manipulate existing text, first highlight the text then apply the formatting).
5. Insert bullets for the three points in paragraph one ("in the seed...", etc.).
6. BOLD the phrase "even in farming" in paragraph one.
7. CUT and PASTE the final sentence moving it to a spot just below the title.
8. SPELLCHECK the document.
9. List the words that were improperly spelled or misused that did not come up in spell check. (Why didn't spell check catch these?)
10. What other problems did you find in PROOFREADING the text?

Technology in Instruction

Whether we like it or not, technology prevails in our society. Even in farming, once the basic framework of our ties too the natural world, we find evidnce of technology: in the seed that has been carefully engineered to produce disease-free crops; in calibrations on farm equipment; in automated the automated process used to record and produce charges for customers' bills at the farm supply store.

The challenge to society becomes how to adequately prepare ourselves for the technological advances we must expect with the advent of the new millenium.

Perhaps the most relevant way to prepare for the infusion of technology is through educational integration. Many college course's provide students with opportunities to use technology for completion of course requirements. Word processing has become an essential sk9ill for any major; students in the sciences are hard pressed if they are not proficient in spreadsheet and data base skills. E-mail and Internet are becoming standard media for communication and research.

Additionally, eductional research becomes more technology intensive every semester. Internet searches have become a standard component for scholars; campus libraries are discontinuing more traditional tools, as the card catalogue, as they place their holdings and databases on line. Traditional research method are insufficient for students competing in today's institutions of higher learning.

The college or university becomes the perfect environment for preparation in use of technology. Students are well served to learn and use technology and virtual communication not as an adjunct too course participation but as integral to the learning process. Faculty must encourage this preparation by making technology a valued coarse component.

Technology is constantly changing, but those with a strong g background in technology applications will have the expertise and confidence to adapt to changes and innovations. While sum may morn the advnces as the loss of a more simple life, those able to employ technology will find themselves well prepared for the rigors of life outside higher education.

Resistance is futile, assimilation inevitable.

Notes:

This exercise can also be used as an introductory diagnostic activity that shows the teacher the relative skill and comfort level of students. Perhaps obviously, teachers should feel free to change the text included above to a text more relevant to specific course goals. In the spirit of the lesson, teachers should be sure to "modify" the text in usefully incorrect ways.

Plan B:

This exercise can also be used with an LCD projector or even an overhead with a transparency. If necessary, teachers could also write the essay on the chalkboard, and have students either copy down the entire text, and then correct it, or simply write the corrected version. Whatever medium the teacher uses, this activity can also be quite productive in small or large group discussions where students can discuss and negotiate the problems and possible solutions to the text.

Select (block), Cut, Copy and Paste

<u>Pedagogical Objective</u>: One distinct advantage to composing using a word processing program is the convenience of quick reordering of text. This activity assists students in understanding the importance of evaluating a paper draft and reorganizing components, adding transitions and connectors.

<u>Technology Skill(s)</u>: SELECT (highlight), COPY, PASTE, and INSERT text.

<u>Process</u>:
1. Following is an essay analyzing a rock song by the Eagles. The paragraphs have been reordered inappropriately and unnecessary information added. Please read through the essay.
2. Using the SELECT, CUT, COPY and PASTE commands, reorganize the essay, eliminate any irrelevant information, and add needed transitions between paragraphs. The paragraphs are numbered for your convenience.

Hotel California

(1) In the song "Hotel California," by the rock band, the Eagles, the issues of a typical mid-life crisis are addressed. The Eagles were a band that had several big hits even though many people objected to their lyrics. Almost every man in America comes to a point where he feels all alone and that the whole world has turned against him. Then the man chooses a way out, something to free him from life. How the man feels about himself after he chooses a path of escape determines whether or not he will conquer his crisis or be conquered by it.

(2) In the first stanza, the protagonist of the song, an average American man, comes to a dead end. He can no longer find any meaning in his boring, mediocre life. He seems to be heading down an endless road, "on a dark desert highway," but he can't seem to find an exit. He is utterly and completely alone. But, then something begins to entice him out of his loneliness, the "warm smell of chaletas." At first he tries to ignore the enticement, but it keeps calling him. The final enticement, the "shimmering light," causes him to give up his fight. He is tired of fighting against himself and the world. He must "stop for the night," so he advances to find out if he can find refuge in the Hotel California. The Eagles used the name of a fictitious hotel for this song.

(3) This song was written during the 1970's, which fact is crucial to the theme of the work. Many men during that time found refuge in drugs, but they eventually paid for their actions. In the song the man comes to a dead end, finds refuge in drugs, and then regrets his actions. The man has not solved his mid-life crisis, but only made it worse. The Eagles probably composed these lyrics in the hope of deterring others from making similar costly mistakes in their lives.

(4) The man's intended path to salvation has now led him elsewhere. He begins to understand what he has done to himself, that he has become one with the others, all "prisoners of [their] own device." And

so he takes the wrong path, all the way to addiction. He and the others know they are trapped, but try as they might, they "just can't kill the beast" of drug dependency. He ends up "running for the door," to find his "passage back to the place [he] was before," but there is no escape. The drug dealer informs him that "you can check out any time you like, but you can never leave," which translates to mean that he can stop his habit whenever he wants, but inevitably his addiction will call him back. The man's escape route has been cut off, and so he his back where he started, with bigger problems than he ever had before.

(5) The man thinks he has found something that can help him escape. But, he stops to reconsider his intentions, thinking that "this could be heaven or this could be hell." He isn't sure if what he's doing is right, but it is too irresistible, so he gives in. "She" shows him "the way." He has found refuge in the "tiffany twisted" world of drugs and materialism. He sees others that have also found in drugs a refuge, where "some dance to remember, some dance to forget." He is doing drugs to forget about his problems, but he sees some others using them to remember the good times. He has divested himself in this endeavor. His drug dealer, the "captain" has enticed the man into addiction, and it seems that he cannot function without this drug. He has returned to the days of peace and love, the "spirit" of 1969 and believes that he is "free" of all responsibilities. But he begins to realize that the drug has taken over his body, since their "voices" still call him from "far away." Some people say the Eagles experimented with drugs and that is the basis of this song.

Notes:

This assignment assumes that teachers can distribute the lesson through some sort of shared folder or network folder. Teachers without access to a LAN could also e-mail this to students as an ATTACHMENT, or post the assignment to a Web page.

Teachers are encouraged to replace the provided essay with something topical or relevant to a current assignment.

Plan B:

This exercise can also be used with an LCD projector or even an overhead with a transparency. If necessary, teachers an also just write the essay on the chalkboard, and have students either copy down the entire text, and then correct it, or simply write the corrected version. Whatever presentation medium the teacher uses, this activity can also be quite productive in small or large group discussions where students can discuss and negotiate the problems and possible solutions to the text.

Works Cited Information Collection

<u>Pedagogical Objective</u>: Researchers are wise to record information about all sources that they investigate during a research project. By recording the information electronically, writers have an accurate record of sources that can be relocated if needed and quickly copied to form a works cited page. This activity starts at the beginning of the research process and concludes with the final draft. It provides direction for recording relevant information on sources and copying and pasting those sources into a works cited page needed for the completed research paper.

<u>Technology Skill(s)</u>: COPY and PASTE.

<u>Process</u>:
Data Collection
1. Create a new blank document, and SAVE the file as "Project Sources."
2. Record relevant information in Project Sources file. You should include the following:
    - Author
    - Title of article/chapter and journal/book
    - Publishing information
    - Volume number, date
    - Page numbers
3. URL and date(s) of Web site (include date of publication if included, last update, and date accessed).
4. Annotated bibliography: Include a brief (three or four sentence) description of the information provided by the source. This makes the source more useful.
5. Check the MLA guide for proper format for citation for articles, book chapters, and the Columbia style for Internet sources. Always keep sources in proper MLA or Columbia formats.
6. Update and SAVE this file after each research session. Include all materials considered, even if some seem initially irrelevant; if the researcher takes a different tack, the irrelevant items may be useful.

Final product
1. Open the "Project Sources" file.
2. Place an asterisk (*) in front of all sources actually cited in the final draft.
3. Scan through the marked entries; decide on the proper order for the citations (alphabetical order by author); replace the * with a number indicating where that entry will appear alphabetically.
4. With the sources file still open, open a new document. SAVE AS "Works Cited."
5. COPY each marked citation in order, being careful not to include the annotation (unless required for the project) and PASTE them into the Works Cited file.
6. Continue to COPY and PASTE until all cited sources are in the new file.
7. Once all files are copied, delete the numbers and do any reformatting necessary to conform to MLA or Columbia standards.

Notes:
Classes using full-featured word processors may want to include hyperlinked Internet resources when possible. In other words, if students find resources on the Internet, some word processors allow the student to create an active hyperlink to that resource from within their word-processed paper. When read on a computer with the correct version of the word processor AND an active Internet connection, clicking on the hyperlinked text would open a Web browser to the appropriate location. Teachers should look through the HELP menu of their word processor to see if it offers hyperlinks, and to see how to create hyperlinks of it does. We recommend the Columbia style citation for electronic sources.

Plan B:
This activity is an extended enterprise that is designed to occur over the length of the research project. Classes with infrequent or unreliable access to computers may want to conduct this exercise using print instead of electronic means. Students create notecards for citations; this is a valuable and time-tested process with which every writing teacher is probably familiar.

Spellcheck Journal

Pedagogical Objective: The spellcheck feature can be a useful learning device that allows students to track their individual spelling problems. This spellcheck activity requires students to check their own papers and record their spelling errors in a provided table. Reuse the activity throughout the semester, having students compare spellcheck tables from paper to paper as a means to track spelling patterns. Students may find, too, that they have patterns in their typos, so this element may be added once students are comfortable with the process.

Technology Skill(s): Spellcheck, COPY and PASTE between documents.

Process:
1. Open your essay.
2. Open this spell table document.
3. Resize both documents (access the HELP menu if necessary).
4. Spellcheck the essay.
5. For each spelling error (don't worry about typos for now) SELECT and COPY the misspelling from the essay into the table below, and then look up and write the correct spelling into the provided column.
    To add more rows to the table:
    - Place your cursor anywhere in the table.
    - Right click the mouse; a menu will pop up.
    - Select INSERT ROWS.
6. Now proofread the essay, paying particular attention to homonyms; that is, to instances of the wrong word, such as "their" for "there." When you find such words, select and copy them into the left hand column of the table, but instead of writing down the correct spelling of the word, write down the definition of EACH of the homonyms being confused in the middle column.

Title of Paper:		Date:
Misspelling	Correct Spelling (or definition)	Number of times misspelled (or misused) in this document

Notes:
This assignment assumes that teachers can distribute the lesson through some sort of shared folder or network folder. Teachers without access to a LAN could also e-mail this to students as an ATTACHMENT, or post the assignment to a Web page (as an FTP link to a word-processing file). This assignment also assumes that the teacher knows how to create a table in a word processor, so teachers who feel a bit rusty using this skill should look over the HELP menu.

Plan B:
Though this exercise does depend rather largely on technology to provide spell checking, teachers might adapt it for a traditional environment by dividing students into groups of three and have committee-style spell-check discussions. Each student would create three grids, and then exchange and read each other's paper. As they read each of their peer's texts, they fill out one of the grids, checking for both misspellings and misused homonyms, and hand them to the author when finished. When the author receives both peer grids, they look up each of the spelling errors identified. If the author's spelling or usage was in fact erroneous, they write that word and its correction on the remaining grid. If the word or usage was correct in the first place, the student should circle that item on the grid given to them by that group member, and give it back to that student at the end of the class. At the end of the exercise, each student should possess all three of their original grids: one with the spelling and usage errors from their own paper as identified by themselves and their peers, and both of the grids they created for their group members, who have circled the words they mistakenly identified as incorrect.

Charting Personal Writing Problems

<u>Pedagogical Objective</u>: Students frequently spend little time seriously reviewing the comments teachers and peers offer on their written work. This writing grid offers an opportunity for students to track their errors and begin to see connections among papers and patterns in their personal writing habits. Requiring the final commentary helps students articulate their "I never realized I did that" discoveries.

<u>Technology Skill(s)</u>: Maneuvering within and manipulating a table.

<u>Process</u>:
  A. Use the following grid to chart the writing problems identified through peer and teacher evaluation on your papers to date. A series of common writing problems have been identified for you; use the empty cells at the bottom to record any problems that do not appear on the chart. In the middle column, record which paper the problems appear in (1,2,3 etc.). The final column is for the number of times you found this problem in your papers.
  B. Review the grid. Can you start seeing a pattern in the errors you make? Write a paragraph summarizing your findings.
  C. Save this grid to disk. Refer back to it (a) when writing the next paper and (b) to record comments from subsequent course papers.

Writing Problem:	Paper:	No. of occurrences:
Noun/verb agreement		
Noun/pronoun agreement		
Comma fault		
Misused semicolon		
Sentence fragment		
Passive voice		

  4. Summary statement: (Include commentary on your most common errors and list some possible strategies for correcting these problems in future papers).

<u>Notes</u>:
This is a great exercise to include in a final portfolio, as it displays and reinforces revision processes. Teachers and students should add to the list their particular "favorites" as needed.

<u>Plan B</u>:
Perhaps obviously, if classes have infrequent or unreliable computer access, this exercise can be completed on paper as easily as on the computer, especially in conjunction with review or peer response exercises.

Peer Interviews for a Case Study

Pedagogical Objective: Students frequently do not anticipate what type of information can be solicited from an interview and often are uncomfortable because they are inexperienced with requesting information from another person. A mock interview provides practice asking (and answering) questions and helps students form an awareness of how people might respond to their questions (giving unexpected answers, not having an opinion, not covering the question fully).

Technology skill(s): Students work in a table to record their answers; the table cells help to separate the answers and thus the elements of the interview. Through the COPY and PASTE commands, students can accurately and quickly capture direct quotations for their sample interview paper.

Process:
1. Choose two of your peers to interview and conduct separate interviews for each using the questions listed below.
2. Complete the provided grid by recording interviewee's answers. Record direct quotations whenever possible.
3. Write two paragraphs summarizing your response to each interview (two paragraphs for each interview). Include such information as how you might have improved your delivery of the questions, what follow-up questions you might have pursued to get more information on a topic, how the interview subject did or did not provide the types of answers you were anticipating.
4. Select one of the interviews and write a short interview paper. Use at least three direct quotes in your piece. COPY and PASTE the quotes from the grid into your commentary.

Interview Questions:
1. How did you feel about your writing before English 103? What types of writing did you do before this class?
2. What invention activity do you feel is the most effective? Why do you think this activity works best for you?
3. Identify which of the following you find the most and the least useful in the process of revising your papers and explain why this is so.
    a. computer lab peer reviews
    b. in-class peer reviews
    c. peer group conferences in the library
    d. peer group conferences during the class period
    e. using the Writing Center or people outside of class to review your paper
    f. reverse outlines
    g. working on individual paragraphs
    h. reading sample essays
    i. teacher comments
4. Do you think the feedback from your peers helped you in revising your papers? How might the group have been more helpful?
5. Which paper assignment did you feel that you were most successful at? Explain why.

6. Which paper helped you the most to learn about your process of writing? Explain why.
7. How do you feel about yourself as a writer now?

Question	Peer 1 response:	Peer 2 response:
1		
2		
3		
4		
5		
6		
7		

Summary of Interview 1:

Summary of Interview 2:

Practice Interview Paper:

Notes:

    Teachers should divide the class into groups of three. The interview itself can be conducted orally or electronically. Students can use the word processor to conduct interviews by having students SAVE the interview questions to disk and then trading disks. The interviewee writes his or her answers, saves the document and returns the disk to the owner, who COPIES and PASTES answers into the appropriate table cell. Adventurous teachers might experiment by having some groups conduct oral interviews and some conduct electronic interviews, and comparing results.

Plan B:

    This exercise can also be used with an LCD projector or even an overhead with a transparency. If necessary, teachers could also write the questions and the response grid on the chalkboard, and have students copy it down before starting the interview process. The interviews themselves can still be conducted orally or through print.

Problem Solving: Investigating and Recommending Specific Action

Pedagogical Objective: This activity promotes invention by having students explore a problem through answering a series of questions about that topic.

Technology Skill(s): Basic word-processing.

Process:
Open a new blank word-processing document, and write each of the following eight questions down. Respond to each step of the heuristic to explore the problem you have selected for this project. Read the sample responses supplied below if you need help getting started or if you are not sure what a question is asking. When you are done, be sure to SAVE the file.

1. Define the problem.
2. Explain why the problem is a problem.
3. Enumerate the goals to be served by a good solution.
4. Rank the goals to be served by the solution according to priority.
5. Outline specific solutions to the problem (at least three).
6. Predict the outcome of each solution.
7. Weigh the predictions in order to determine which solution will achieve the goals given the highest priority earliest.
8. Appraise what appears to be the best solution. In other words, evaluate the set of procedures that seems best suited to reaching the most important goals.

SAMPLE PROBLEM

The existing final exam policy on campus should be changed.

1. This problem focuses on a conflict between what final exams are supposed to accomplish and what they actually do. These exams are supposed to give students a chance to bring together all of the most important things they have learned that semester. Professors are supposed to find out from a final examination exactly how much of a course's material students have learned. But because of all the pressure and the limited time students have to take exams, they many not be able to show all that they have learned, and professors don't get a very good idea about how much students know about the subject after studying it for a semester.

2. Final exams are a problem because they make everyone feel like too much of a failure at the end of the semester. The students don't have a chance to show what they have really learned, and they get grades that make it seem as if they all know less than they do. Professors feel cheated because they have worked hard all semester to teach students something, and final exams seem to say that students haven't learned as much as they should have. So, the professor's time seems wasted. Everybody ends up feeling like a loser.

3. Some system should be used to test students' knowledge at the end of a course. But it shouldn't include conditions that work against students' really showing what they have learned. There should be a balance between what students are expected to do and what conditions allow them to do. And whatever system is used, it should be good enough to reveal what students have actually learned and teachers have actually taught.

4. All three of these goals are equally important, and you can't achieve one without achieving the other two.

5. Students should be tested at the end of a semester because no one can really know how much they have learned if they are not tested. But the tests they are given should not be picky. Final exams should ask about the most important topics covered in a course. Students should also not be asked to finish a final exam in a short period of time. If they are going to be stating all that they have learned in a course, they should be able to relax and respond to questions at an easier pace than most final exam schedules allow. Two ways to do this would be to give them take-home exams or to let them take exams in class over a period of two or three days. Both of these might require a longer final exam period, but going from a one-week final exam period to a two- or three-week final exam period should be acceptable if this eliminated all of the problems that students experience under the system now. Giving students the chance to take final exams at an easier pace would give them and their teachers a real chance to know what they have accomplished that semester. If students could not answer the questions they are given, they couldn't use the excuse that they didn't have enough time. Teachers would be helped by the system because they could see what most students in their classes did and did not learn.

6. The hardest part of figuring out a good system for final exams is coming up with something that doesn't have any loopholes. The big problem with letting students do take-home exams is that this may allow them to help each other out more than the professor wants them to. If this happens, no one is any better off than before because students who cheat don't need to learn, and if they get better grades than they should, the professor still doesn't know how effective he has been. Even the majority of students who don't cheat would be hurt because the ones who did cheat would ruin the curve, and the ones who didn't would get grades that are lower than they should be. This still could be a good solution, though, if the professor could make up a take-home exam that students couldn't cheat on.

Having students take in-class exams over a two- or three-day period might be a better solution because it would give a more accurate indication of how well everyone in class really did. The big drawback to this arrangement is that it would take more time and probably more money. This would probably mean that the final exam period would have to be stretched from one week to two weeks. It wouldn't have to take more time and more money if the people who run universities agreed to eliminate one week of regular classes in order to have two weeks of final exams. Even though a week of classes would be lost, the gains that would be made in making final exams a real learning experience and a true measure of what students have learned would more than make up for the lost class time.

7. Giving students take-home final exams could create a situation in which the students and the teacher might not be able to tell from the results how well they performed over a semester. Maybe this difficulty could be overcome, but maybe it couldn't. However, stretching the final exam period from one to two weeks and having students take a final exam for a specific course of two or three exam sessions would meet all of the goals that a good solution should meet. Most of all, it would create a situation in which students would be able to take a final exam under reasonable conditions, and, when it was all over, the students and the teacher would be able to know from the results of the exam how successful they were that semester.

8. Having students take final exams over two or three class sessions has the added advantage of increasing the chances that they would remember what they had learned for a longer period of time than they would if they had to cram. So, this system would not only make a final exam a better indication of what students and teachers have actually accomplished, it would also have an effect on students that would help them to succeed more in the future.

Notes:
This exercise is designed to be used in conjunction with an argument or position paper. If students do not already have topics, teachers might want to assign topics, provide a list of possible topics, and/or spend a few minutes at the beginning of class to brainstorm some topics to use with this exercise.

Plan B:
This exercise can also be done using handouts or a chalkboard.

Rewriting Exercise

<u>Pedagogical Objective</u>: To encourage students to do a major revision of a draft, giving the paper a different slant. This activity illustrates that no draft is final and offers a procedure for systematically "shaking up" a draft that might seem staid and settled.

<u>Technological Skill(s)</u>: Splitting screens and transferring text from one document to another.

<u>Process</u>:
Task 1: Creating New Paragraphs
1. Begin by rewriting your thesis statement in a new blank document.
2. Write new topic sentences, based on your original paragraphs, that directly relate to your new thesis.
3. Finally, freewrite paragraphs for the new topic sentences, taking a new or different angle.

Task 2: Revising Old Paper
1. Make second copies of both your original paper and your new paragraphs, saved under different file names.
2. Split your screen (See the HELP menu for instructions. If necessary, simply OPEN both documents and switch between screens).
3. Combine the two documents by adding what new information you want to preserve from the original document to the new paragraphs by cutting and pasting.
4. At the same time, put any sentences from the new paragraphs that you do not want to keep into the original document, which will become an "early version" file.
5. SAVE the revised document under a new name.

<u>Notes</u>:
   This exercise is particularly useful for illustrating the reflexive nature of composition. It can be usefully combined with a peer revision/response kind of exercise to give students feedback on the choices they made and the effective differences between versions of their papers; they might realize that such rewriting can be useful.

<u>Plan B</u>:
   This exercise can also be accomplished using good old pencil and paper. Use of a copy machine, some scissors, and some tape or glue will greatly facilitate the second step of the exercise.

Chapter 13

Lesson Plans Using E-mail

This chapter includes a number of lesson plans designed to be used with e-mail; as in Chapter 12, we do not claim to present an exhaustive list, but rather, hope to illustrate some principles of using e-mail in class through specific examples.

The use of e-mail in class can be broadly organized into two categories based upon audience: local and public. Local assignments ask students to compose e-mail messages that do not pass beyond the borders of the virtual classroom. Such assignments include messages written between students, between students and the teacher, and messages that are not sent to anyone, or which are sent only to the writer. Public assignments include any exercise that asks a student to communicate with someone outside the borders of the virtual classroom, such as an interview, participation in a public newsgroup or mailing list, or a letter written to a newspaper or local government office.

Each of these assignment types require different preparation by the teacher, but all require that each student, as well as the teacher, has his or her own e-mail account active and working. We recommend that teachers standardize e-mail platforms as much as possible; if each student in the class is using a different e-mail program, teachers will find many unexpected problems and will be unable to teach any specific e-mail processes. Students who are very familiar with a particular e-mail program should be allowed to continue using that program wherever possible (comfortable writing spaces are not so common that teachers can afford to discard one), but students who are unfamiliar with e-mail or who do not express a strong preference should be encouraged to use a single standardized e-mail program for class.

Local e-mail assignments are easy to set up, but an initial step might be the creation of a mass mail list for the course. Such a list is very easy to set up. As soon as possible during the semester, teachers should ask students to e-mail them something. The content of this message is immaterial, but the enterprising teacher might have students write a diagnostic essay in the e-mail. Regardless, the purpose of this e-mail is to allow the teacher to gather actual e-mail addresses of his or her students. When the teacher receives these messages, he or she should create an address book for the class (teachers should access the HELP menu in their e-mail program for specifics on how to set up and manipulate address books). Teachers who create Web sites for their class can also create a mass mail link off a Web page (see Chapter 9 for more information about using the Web for class). This mass e-mail list can be used to distribute assignments, send out important messages to the entire class or to selected students (and thus create small group mailing lists), or to provide a virtual large group discussion in which everyone can see and respond to each step in the conversation. Teachers can ask students to create their own address books as well and transfer some of the administrative duties onto the students themselves. Either way, once students have a single e-mail message that has everyone's e-mail address included, they can always e-mail the entire class by hitting "REPLY" to that message. Teachers who want to use these kinds of mass mail tools for their class should supply the infrastructure by sending an introductory message to the entire class as early in the semester as possible, and put something like "mass mail addresses" in the subject line.

Even better, teachers could use a newsgroup or mailing list for their class. As discussed in Chapter 5, both newsgroups and mailing lists are ways to centralize and distribute information to each student in the class, and alleviates the need to create mass mail links or address book files. Both media are easy to use, but teachers will have to check with their school's technology coordinator or lab supervisor to set up these tools before the beginning of the semester.

Public e-mail assignments require a bit more work on the part of the teacher because of netiquette and common courtesy (see Appendix C for a brief discussion of netiquette). In particular, teachers should not just unleash their students on an unsuspecting target. Letters written to public officials or newspapers might be exceptions, but in general, teachers should write any outside parties before the start of the semester and make sure they agree to participate in the exercise. Some authors even agree to interviews or presentations on a book they wrote or a topic of personal interest.

Because e-mail comprises what amounts to very mobile word-processing documents, most of the assignments presented in Chapter 12 can be adapted for use with e-mail. Most e-mail programs[24] allow users to CUT, COPY and PASTE, so students can work on those kinds of assignments in an e-mail screen, or even COPY a document from a word processor and PASTE it into e-mail (depending on the length of the document -- texts longer than a few pages should be sent as an ATTACHMENT).

Many of the exercises included in this chapter are designed to be SENT to students (that is, for teachers to use e-mail as a "class assignment" document). We recommend that teachers develop a naming protocol for such assignments, and use such names in the subject line of the e-mail messages. For example, a teacher might use a system like "Assignment [date]" in the subject line, so that students receiving the e-mail will know to read that message right away.

---

[24] UNIX-based server-side e-mail programs usually do not support COPY and PASTE functions.

Diagnostic Exercise

<u>Pedagogical Objective</u>: This exercise is designed to be used early in the semester, and can be used as a diagnostic activity. The questions can be modified to more specific writing prompts if the exercise is used later in the semester, or if the students are familiar with word-processing and e-mail.

<u>Technology Skill(s)</u>: E-mail basics: compose and SEND.

<u>Process</u>:
1. Open a new e-mail composition window.
2. In the "to" field, type my e-mail address *(teacher@school.edu)*. Remember that you must type my address exactly. Do not add spaces, change spelling, capitalization, or punctuation.
3. In the "CC" field, type in your own e-mail address. Again, be careful to write it exactly as it should appear, or the message will not be sent.
4. In the "Subject" line, write "Introduction."
5. In the main body of the message, write a paragraph that describes the kind of experience you have using computers. Please include the following information:
   - Your actual name (as it appears on my class roster).
   - Your preferred e-mail address.
   - Which word processor you normally use to write papers.
   - How often you use e-mail and to whom you normally write.
   - Your experience using the World Wide Web (even if you have never "browsed" the Web, you probably have friends who do, or have read and seen references to Web in the newspaper or on television -- please write about your general impression of the Web).
   - What kind of computer system you normally use.
   - What you normally use the computer for (writing papers, e-mail, Web, games, etc.).
   - How you would rate yourself as a computer user (Luddite, novice, casual user, experienced user, geek, hacker).
6. When you are finished, please read over the paragraph you have written, and proofread it carefully for spelling and punctuation errors.
7. Finally, SEND the document.
8. Click the "Get new messages" button. You should receive your copy in a minute or two (at most). If you receive a message from the MAILER DAEMON your mail did not get sent successfully for some reason. Please raise your hand and a lab technician or I will be over to help you figure out what went wrong.

Notes:
If teachers use this exercise in the beginning of the semester, they may wish to write it on a whiteboard, use an overhead projector, or even make a printed handout for the students. This exercise is provides an excellent opportunity for students to access the HELP menu of the e-mail program the class is using to learn the particulars of sending and receiving e-mail. Teachers should ask the lab attendant for extra help during this exercise, as any problems with student e-mail accounts are likely to appear.

Plan B:
Because this exercise is designed to introduce students to e-mail, there is no real "Plan B." Certainly, students can write out and hand in their answers using a word processor or pencil and paper, but that sort of defeats the purpose of the exercise.

E-mail Discussion

<u>Pedagogical Objective</u>: This exercise asks students to write responses to an article or reading, and then send those responses via e-mail into a class discussion area.

<u>Technology Skill(s)</u>: Basic e-mail: compose, REPLY, SEND.

<u>Process</u>:
1. Before doing anything else, please read through this entire assignment.
2. Click on the "REPLY TO ALL" button.
3. Read the paragraph below (taken from William Wordsworth's "Preface to Lyrical Ballads" -- You can find the complete text at <http://www.english.upenn.edu/~mgamer/Romantic/lbprose.html#preface>, but for the purposes of this in-class assignment, you can use the following excerpt).
4. Please answer the following questions (you can include your answers below the questions in your e-mail REPLY):
   - According to Wordsworth, what differentiates the poet from other men?
   - What do you think Wordsworth means when he writes that the poet has "a more comprehensive soul" than most other men?
   - Wordsworth uses the term "men" in this paragraph. Do you think he was referring to men specifically, or was he using the term to include women as well? Do you think the gender of a poet is important? Why or why not?
   - In a short paragraph, answer the question, "What is a poet"?
5. When you are finished answering the questions, please SEND your message.
6. For homework, please read through at least three of your classmates' answers. We will continue this discussion during the next class period.

READING
(an excerpt from William Wordsworth's "Preface to Lyrical Ballads")

What is a poet? [. . .] He is a man speaking to men: a man, it is true, endued with more lively sensibility, more enthusiasm and tenderness, who has a greater knowledge of human nature, and a more comprehensive soul, than are supposed to be common among mankind; a man pleased with his own passions and volitions, and who rejoices more than other men in the spirit of life that is in him; delighting to contemplate similar volitions and passions as manifested in the goings-on of the universe, and habitually impelled to create them where he does not find them. To these qualities he has added a disposition to be affected more than other men by absent things as if they were present; an ability of conjuring up in himself passions, which are indeed far from being the same as those produced by real events.

Notes:
This assignment is designed to be sent to students via e-mail before class (or posted to the class newsgroup). If teachers use this lesson early in the semester, they might need to remind students how to get into their e-mail, and how to recognize assignments sent through e-mail via the subject line as well as the "From" field.

The exercise works best if the class has a newsgroup or mailing list in place to distribute both the assignment and students' e-mail responses to each other. If such tools are unavailable, the teacher can use a mass mail link or an address book list to send the assignment to each student through e-mail.

Teachers should use readings germane to their class schedule, and the response prompts should be designed with the pedagogical objective in mind. The reading included above is only an example, though teachers should feel free to use it if they wish.

Readings can be accessed in several ways. Because this sample document is short, we have included it as part of the e-mail message. If it were longer, we might have included it as an ATTACHMENT. If it were posted on the Web, we might just supply a URL. If it were a print document, of course, we could just refer to the reading, and assume (hope) that students have brought their material to class.

Plan B:
Perhaps obviously, students can also use pencil and paper for this assignment if the technology is being uncooperative.

Introductions

Pedagogical Objective: Students write short introductions of themselves, and share these descriptions to the class. This is a good exercise early in the semester, as an icebreaker, or simply as a way to reinforce the (virtual) writing community.

Technology Skill(s): Basic e-mail: compose, SEND. Potential advanced e-mail skills if students want to include pictures or other special elements to their introduction.

Process:
1. Open a new e-mail window and address it to the class*
2. Write an introduction of yourself to the class, focussing on how you see yourself as a writer. This text should represent you, so feel free to be as formal or playful as you wish in how you write it, but remember that this introduction will be sent to everyone, and they can SAVE or PRINT them. So don't go nuts. Please use the prompts below to help you get started.
   - What kinds of things do you write (papers, notes, poems, e-mail, Web pages, programming code, shopping lists)?
   - What is the best thing you have ever written? Tell us a little bit about what you wrote, and why you wrote it.
   - What is your favorite place to write?
   - Do you have any special writing rituals (silence, music, special pens, customized toolbars)?
3. When you are finished writing your introduction, please read over it again, and check for spelling and grammar errors. If you find any, please fix them (remember to make a good first impression on your fellow classmates!).
4. SEND the document.
5. During the balance of the period, or for homework, please read through your classmates' introductions. Pick your favorite introduction: we'll begin class next time by talking about the introductions we liked, and why.

Notes:
*This exercise assumes the existence of a class newsgroup, mailing list, or mass mail tool, because the introductions are supposed to be publicly posted.

Depending upon the e-mail program used in class, special elements such as pictures can be included in this Introduction. Many popular e-mail programs now allow users to send and receive e-mail written HTML. This means that users can include in their e-mail most of what one can find on a Web page (pictures, hyperlinks, animations, etc.). Of course, this is only partially accurate -- the e-mail message being sent is actually the HTML file (see Chapter 9 for more information), and any pictures or sounds are sent as ATTACHMENTS to the e-mail.

Plan B:
    There is not a satisfactory low-tech equivalent to this exercise.

Holiday Season Rituals

Pedagogical Objective: This exercise asks students to conduct a series of interviews with each other designed to explore winter season holiday rituals, such as those associated with Christmas, Hanukkah, or Kwanza.

Technology Skill(s): Basic e-mail: compose, REPLY, SEND, saving messages.

Process:
1. Open a new e-mail window. In the body of the message, freewrite for 10 minutes about some of the rituals you and your family perform during the winter holiday season, such as making cookies, singing holiday songs, feasting, shopping, or visiting relatives.
2. When the ten minutes is up, choose a partner and exchange e-mail addresses.
3. Now shape your freewriting into something resembling a structured e-mail letter. The goal here is to provide your partner with some information to start with, so focus on one or two of the things you wrote about in your freewriting. Your partner will be asking you for more details about the rituals, so you don't have to be too specific or complete at this point.
4. SEND the message to your partner.
5. When you receive your partner's message, read through it, making notes about the rituals described, and paying special attention to the ways in which those rituals are different from your own.
6. REPLY to your partner's message by asking him or her 5 questions. These questions should be designed to gather more information about the rituals and about how your partner feels about them. Here are some ideas to get you started:
   - What do you know about the history of your ritual?
   - What is your strongest specific memory of your ritual?
   - How do you think your ritual fits into our overall holiday experience?

   (Yes, I only gave you three ideas. You'll have to think up at least a couple on your own. Notice that each question is open-ended: they cannot be answered by a simple yes or no. Good questions prompt the interviewee to open up and really start talking to you.)
7. SEND your reply to your partner.
8. Answer the questions your partner has sent you. Try to be forthcoming and helpful, and give your interviewer the information he or she is asking for. When you are done, please SEND it off.
9. Once you get your partner's responses to the questions you asked, please read through them. Ask yourself the following questions:
   - Do you enough about the ritual to perform it yourself if you wanted?
   - Do you know what the ritual means to your partner?
   - What do you still not know about the ritual? (You can write your answers to these questions if you'd like, but you don't have to).
10. Again, hit REPLY to the message, and ask 3 more questions, based upon your answers, or rather, remaining questions, from step 9.

11. Answer the questions your partner has sent you. When you are done, please SEND them back to your partner.
12. When you get your partner's responses, you should now have a document containing your partner's original text, and your partner's answers to all eight questions (the first five, and then the second three) you have asked. Based on the information in this document, write a short paper describing the holiday ritual in question. Use quotes from the interview wherever appropriate.

Notes:

This multi-class period lesson puts students in pairs to conduct interviews, but small groups (3 or 4) can also be used. For small groups, students should send each message to the whole group (using a simple mass mail link, address book, or by manually typing in each e-mail address into the "To" field). Students in the groups should increase the number of questions they ask by one in each phase (6 and 4, respectively), and split them between all the members of the group. The resulting paper can be a comparison or contrast paper that looks at each of the different rituals.

Teachers might also consider having students interview people outside the classroom using this basic lesson design. We recommend that teachers provide a specific set of guidelines to students about who to interview, and the proper (and courteous) way to set up an interview with someone.

Plan B:

This lesson can easily be done on pencil and paper instead of e-mail, or through oral conversations.

Small Group Brainstorming and Topic Selection

Pedagogical Objective: To have small groups of students brainstorm and expand paper topics.

Technology Skill(s): Basic e-mail: compose, SEND, REPLY in small groups.

Process:
As always, please read through the entire assignment before doing anything else.
1. Open a new e-mail document, and address it to your small group.
2. In the subject line, write down a topic you are thinking of using for the next paper.
3. SEND your message to the group.
4. Before doing anything else, freewrite about your topic for 5 minutes, focusing on associations (in other words, what other topics does your topic raise?). You can write this in another e-mail window or on paper.
5. Read the topics from your group members and REPLY to each document. For each, write for about 5 minutes about the topic that they have suggested, again focusing on associations. Don't worry if you don't know very much about their topic; part of the point of this exercise is to generate ideas from different perspectives. Write about what that topic means to you.
6. SEND each reply when you are finished freewriting.
7. By the time your group finishes this part of the exercise, each group member should have a list of ideas about their topic from each person in the group.
8. Using the COPY and PASTE functions, consolidate these documents into one long list, eliminating any duplicate associations.
9. SEND this list to the group. (Remember to include yourself if you want to save a copy).
10. REPLY to each of these lists sent by your group, this time eliminating unnecessary or irrelevant associations or ideas. Your goal here is to help your group members focus and sharpen their topic, so give them your honest opinion. Remember, a good topic holds the reader's interest, and can realistically and adequately be discussed in a few pages. Please SEND these replies back as soon as you finish each.
11. At the end of this exercise, each group member should have a topic that has been expanded and then re-focused from several different sources. Please SAVE or PRINT these documents, as I will collect them as part of your final portfolio.
12. For homework, begin working on an outline, using your group's suggestions about your topic as a springboard for your paper.

Notes:
      This exercise assumes the use of small groups. Teachers can set up small e-mail groups in several ways, but the easiest is probably to have students exchange addresses in class and send e-mail to everyone in their group.

Plan B: This lesson works well using pencil, paper, and oral discussion. Students merely trade pieces of paper rather than use e-mail.

Writing for Different Audiences

Pedagogical Objective: To help students become aware of audience, medium, and how their writing changes according to the expected reader.

Technology Skill(s): Basic e-mail, CUT, COPY and PASTE, light multi-tasking (e-mail and word-processing).

Process:
1. Find a partner and exchange e-mail addresses. For the purposes of this assignment, one of you will be student A and the other student B.
2. You will be writing two letters. The first letter will be written to your roommate (or friend), and the second one to a potential employer in Washington. You have spoken or written to both audiences before, and both want to know how you are doing in school.
3. Student A should write the first letter on paper, and the second as an e-mail. Student B should write the first letter as an e-mail, and the second on paper. Remember that the subject for each letter is the same.
4. When you are done writing both letters, exchange them with your partner.
5. When you get your partner's letters, read them both through, then in a separate e-mail window (addressed to your partner, yourself, and to me), answer the following questions:
   - How did the difference in audience change the content of the letter?
   - Was there a difference in tone between the two letters? If so, please explain what that difference was.
   - Did the actual structure of the letter change because of audience (headings, date, other formal or informal conventions of letter-writing? Please explain in detail.
   - What differences did the medium have upon the content, tone, or structure of the letters (you may have to re-read your letters to answer this question)? In other words, you and your partner each wrote two letters to the same two people, but used different media to do so -- what difference, if any, did that make?
6. When you are finished answering these questions, go ahead and SEND it off. (Remember that you should get a copy of it).
7. Once your partner replies to you and you have your own letters back, read through the answers your partner wrote.

Notes:

Teachers who want to expand upon this lesson may want to have students role-play the audience and formulate a reaction to one or both of the letters. This expansion can be useful in reinforcing the students' sense of audience, and can be a lot of fun at the same time.

Alternately, teachers may wish to make the "public" letter an actual rather than pretend audience. Teachers who wish to pursue this option should find friendly administrators, librarians, public officials, or professors willing to participate in the exercise before the beginning of the class, and make sure they know what they are getting themselves into.

Plan B:
This exercise, as written, depends upon technology. Teachers might be able to achieve a similar effect by having students write print documents for different audiences; students might be assigned "personalities" in small groups, and do a role-playing type response to the letters. Obviously, such an adaptation would need to drop the media comparison element of the exercise.

Individual/ Small Group "Oral" Reports

<u>Pedagogical Objective</u>: This exercise takes the traditional oral report and puts it on-line. The pedagogical objectives remain unchanged for the most part, but students are asked to communicate their findings in writing, and to mediate the e-mail discussion that follows.

<u>Technology Skill(s)</u>: Basic e-mail: compose, SEND, REPLY.

<u>Process</u>:
1. You or your group should write your report in an e-mail message sent to the entire class (via newsgroup, mailing list, or mass mail link). Your report should be sent to the class no later than 24 hours before your presentation. Your presentation should conclude with no fewer than three discussion prompts (related topics, elements of your presentation that might need development or discussion, points of your presentation that are controversial).
2. At the beginning of the class period, audience members should carefully read the presentation.
3. Each audience member should compose a REPLY to the presentation. Students should feel free to reply in any constructive manner, but can use the discussion prompts included in the presentation as a starting point.
4. When the reply is finished, audience members should SEND the message back to the class.
5. You (and your group, if applicable) should wait until everyone has had a chance to reply to the presentation, and then facilitate the discussion by answering questions posed by the audience, defending points in your presentation, or asking questions back to your audience.

<u>Notes</u>:
    This project assumes that teachers have integrated this "report" project into their course schedules, and that students will know what they are supposed to be presenting on. Presentations on readings or special topics are fairly standard subjects for traditional oral reports, and also work well in this context. This exercise also works very well using students papers as a basis for discussion, in which case, the lesson becomes something of a group peer feedback session.
    Teachers who wish to expand this exercise might try to use a chat room for the "discussion" phase of the presentation. Chat rooms more closely approximate oral conversation, so audience response tends to be more immediate and often more "spirited" (with both positive and negative potentials). Teachers who wish to pursue this option should discuss with the presenting student(s) how the chat room works, and what will be expected of them in terms of mediating the discussion.

<u>Plan B</u>:
    Perhaps obviously, students should be prepared to go ahead with an actual oral report and discussion if the technology aspect of this exercise becomes problematic for any reason.

Critical "Lurking"

<u>Pedagogical Objective</u>: This exercise asks students to read and evaluate a public discourse without participating in that dialogue. The lesson can be useful as a way to introduce the concept of discourse communities, or the differences between virtual discourse communities and more traditional forums.

<u>Technology Skill(s)</u>: Reading and navigating a newsgroup, mailing list, or message archive.

<u>Process</u>:
1. Choose one of the following newsgroups:
    - alt.usage.english
    - rec.arts.books.childrens
    - misc.writing
    - rec.arts.sf.composition
    - rec.arts.comics.misc
    - humanities.classics
    - alt.conspiracy
2. For the next week, please "lurk" on the newsgroup. Read all the messages that are posted during the week, but do not post anything yourself. These newsgroups are all fairly high volume, so make sure to read all the new messages each day, or you'll get too far behind to catch up.
3. As you read through the newsgroup, please take notes of the following items:
    - How many messages are posted on each day?
    - Of these, how many are new threads? (Remember that a thread is a new topic posted to the group).
    - How many are replies?
    - How many messages are in an average thread?
    - Is there a "core" group of people who post or reply to threads more often than others?
    - What kinds of topics are being discussed?
    - How formal are the postings to the group? (Does spelling and grammar seem to matter? Overtly or implicitly?)
    - Does the group seem to be gendered in important ways? (Do men post more often than women do? Who seems to "control" discussion threads?)
    - Any events or discussions you found unusual or exciting (you might want to SAVE or PRINT these messages).
    - Any outside resource available to the newsgroup (an FAQ, Web site, archives, etc.).
    - Any other information you think might be relevant.
4. Based upon your observations of the newsgroup over the week, compose a report that describes and evaluates the forum, focussing upon the defining characteristics of this discourse community. The audience of this analysis is our class, and should culminate in a recommendation to subscribe to or avoid the newsgroup. Your report should

include as much information from the above questions as possible, and you should use quotes from specific messages whenever appropriate.
5. When you are finished, SEND your report to the class. Your evaluation should be posted no later than [day and time].

Notes:

Even though students are asked not to post messages to these newsgroups, netiquette still suggests that teachers should inform the group moderator of the exercise, and make sure that this "lurking" exercise is acceptable. Though such groups are public, there are still issues of privacy and fair use to be considered, and courtesy requires notification.

The process described above assumes that teachers have picked out specific newsgroups or mailing lists beforehand. Teachers should pick lists with moderate to heavy usage (between 10 and 100 posts during an average week). To find appropriate newsgroups, teachers might want to check out <http://www.dejanews.com/>. For mailing lists, the Public Access Mailing List Web site has a lot of information and a search engine: <http://www.neosoft.com/Internet/paml/>. In any case, teachers may want to have students start with news.announce.newusers -- a newsgroup devoted to explaining newsgroups to new users.

Classes with access to Web browsers may wish to have students find their own newsgroup by using a search engine. This process is fairly standard and straight forward, but teachers should still be very careful about the kinds of discussion groups students are "lurking" on. Some newsgroups are very inappropriate for this kind of exercise (porn lists, other bizarre or offensive lists) -- teachers should make sure they explain guidelines carefully, and should themselves lurk on any forums that seem suspicious or questionable.

Plan B:

Because this lesson focuses so explicitly upon e-mail discussion groups, no traditional classroom equivalent exists (unless teachers have a lot of extra time and money on their hands and wish to print out and copy a week's worth of e-mail messages from a discussion group).

Chapter 14

Web-Based Lesson Plans

Like Chapters 12 and 13, this chapter contains lesson plans that are designed to act as templates. Further, due to the flexible and comprehensive nature of the Web, teachers should consider these lesson plans to be cumulative with those offered in the previous two chapters. In other words, teachers using Web-based lesson plans can use all of the lesson templates provided in Chapter 13, because the Web offers seamless e-mail integration. Therein, teachers can also use most of the lesson templates suggested in Chapter 12, as e-mail offers a very basic word-processing space. We recommend that teachers use Web-based lesson plans if possible, because the Web offers the greatest flexibility and because students have an almost unlimited supply of outside resources at their disposal.

As with e-mail, use of web-based lesson plans can be divided into two main categories: local and public. Local Web assignments do not use any outside resources. In fact, such pages don't even have to be "published" onto an actual web server. All Web pages are potentially hypertextual documents; that is, each file can be linked to other files. The HELP menus in Windows 95 and MacOS are examples of local hypertextual files: they use links to provide easy access between documents, but are not posted onto a public Web server. Teachers can use a local area network to achieve a similar effect by saving their Web documents to a shared network drive or folder to which students have access (see Chapter 4 for more information about using a LAN). Local assignments might ask students to e-mail each other, take a quiz posted by the teacher, or read and respond to a paper posted by a fellow student. Local assignments can run without an active Internet connection.

Public Web assignments are those that use outside resources, such as a search engine, or a Web site posted on a remote server. Public assignments might ask students to find or evaluate a set of resources, take an on-line quiz posted at a remote location, or even "chat" with a student in Ireland. Public web assignments do not necessarily have to be posted on public Web servers, however. In fact, web pages saved on a LAN can use external hyperlinks (links to outside resources); the only difference between pages posted on a LAN and pages published to a Web server is outside access: users can access pages on a Web server from anywhere in the world, while LAN access usually requires the user to be at a specified physical location (such as a computer lab). Assignments that use external resources do require an active Internet connection.

All the lesson plans included below are designed to be posted (accessed) on the Web as "Assignment Pages" (that is, pages that students should automatically read as soon as they get into class). Teachers should feel free to spice up assignment pages with graphics, so long as the pictures don't make the text hard to read, or detract from the message of the text. Chapter 9 discusses some of the ways teachers can use the Web for class, and Appendix C provides teachers some example Web page scripts. The first two lesson plans below are "translations" of exercises presented in Chapters 12 and 13, respectively, and show what the resulting "assignment page" might look like. The third lesson is an example of what an on-line final exam might look like. (The scripts for these lessons are included in Appendix C). The remainder of the lessons is presented through the textual format used in Chapters 12 and 13.

Diagnostic Exercise (version 1)

Congratulations and welcome! Since you are obviously reading this page, you have successfully found our class Web site. This portion of our Web site will normally contain the assignment for the day, so make sure you check it as soon as you get into class. (In fact, you may want to BOOKMARK the page).

Today's assignment is going to be a simple writing activity in which you tell me something about your familiarity with computers. Please follow the directions below, and raise your hand if you have any questions.

Assignment:
Before you do anything, please read through the entire assignment. You'll get lost if you start the assignment without reading all the directions first.
1. CLICK HERE to open an e-mail window.
2. In the e-mail window that pops up, (it will be pre-addressed to me), write a paragraph that describes the kind of experience you have using computers. Please include the following information:
   - Your actual name (as it appears on my class roster).
   - Your preferred e-mail address.
   - Which word processor you normally use to write papers.
   - How often you use e-mail and to whom you normally write.
   - Your experience using the World Wide Web (even if this is it!).
   - What kind of computer system you normally use.
   - What you normally use the computer for (writing papers, e-mail, Web, games, etc.).
   - How you would rate yourself as a computer user (Luddite, novice, casual user, experienced user, geek, guru).
3. When you are finished, please read over the paragraph you have written, and proofread it carefully for spelling and punctuation errors.
4. Finally, SEND the document.

Diagnostic Exercise (version 2)

● Congratulations and welcome! Since you are obviously reading this page, you have successfully found our class Web site. This portion of our Web site will normally contain the assignment for the day, so make sure you check it as soon as you get into class. (In fact, you may want to BOOKMARK the page).

Today's assignment is going to be a simple writing activity in which you tell me something about your familiarity with computers. Please follow the directions below, and raise your hand if you have any questions.

Assignment:
Before you do anything, please read through the entire assignment. You'll get lost if you start the assignment without reading all the directions first.

1. In the text window below, write a paragraph that describes the kind of experience you have using computers. Please include the following information:
- Your actual name (as it appears on my class roster).
- Your preferred e-mail address.
- Which word processor you normally use to write papers.
- How often you use e-mail and to whom you normally write.
- Your experience using the World Wide Web (even if this is it!).
- What kind of computer system you normally use.
- What you normally use the computer for (writing papers, e-mail, Web, games).
- How you would rate yourself as a computer user (Luddite, novice, casual user, experienced user, geek, guru).

2. When you are finished, please read over the paragraph you have written, and proofread it carefully for spelling and punctuation errors.

3. Finally, SUBMIT the document. Hit the RESET Button only if you want to start over.

Your Name: [_____]

Your e-mail address: [_____]

Write your answers below:

[text area]

[Submit] [Reset]

Final Exam

Your Name: [_____]

Instructions:

This exam is a take-home final. You must return it to me by Friday, Dec. 11, at 4PM. All exams MUST be written on a word processor or entered through this form. You should proofread your exam before handing it in (if I see a lot of stupid spelling or grammar errors, I will deduct points from your essay). You must complete this exam on your own -- you may not collaborate with another student. You may go to the writing center if you want help proofreading the document.

Please read through ALL of the questions carefully. You MUST answer question #1. Choose any TWO of the other questions, and answer them. Your answers should be as complete as possible, and should use specific examples from the texts whenever possible.

Questions:

1. Based on the texts we have read and the discussions we have had in class, how would you define satire? What are its necessary elements? (In other words, how can you tell if something is a satire?)

2. While discussing Monty Python's *The Holy Grail*, I suggested that the whole movie is summarized in the opening credits. What led me to make this claim? Do you agree with this statement or not? Support your position with tons of examples and details.

3. What is the purpose of satire? Or, what are some of the purposes of satire? Support your answer by considering and explaining the specific goals and methods of at least three different satires we have read this semester.

4. Compare Gulliver as narrator (from *Gulliver's Travels*) to Jack as Narrator (from *Stinky Cheese Man*). How do they function as narrators? How do these functions relate to the satire of the text? Do these functions change through the course of the text, or do their narrative functions remain consistent? How does this change, or lack thereof, relate to the vehicle of the satire?

5. Compare *South Park* and *Alice in Wonderland*. Both comment on "Childhood" in some ways, and both react against what they perceive to be a stifling cultural environment. What are these "environments" that

the satire reacts against? How does each text manipulate that environment? How would you identify the goal of each satire? Why are these texts read so differently today?

[ ]

6. Compare the use of vehicle in Monty Python's *The Holy Grail* and *Stinky Cheese Man*. (Be specific).

[ ]

7. Many of the satires we have read this semester involve the ability of language to communicate effectively. Choose three examples, and explain how these texts satirize language, and why.

[ ]

8. Several of the satires we have read question cultural assumptions, stereotypes and myths. Pick one such assumption, stereotype or myth, and compare its satirical treatment in at least three of the texts we have read in class.

[ ]

EXTRA CREDIT
What is your quest?

[ ]

When you are finished, hit the "submit final" button. Remember to proofread your work first.

[Submit Final] [Reset]

Citation Style Treasure Hunt

Pedagogical Objective: This is a wonderful exercise that asks students to find specific things on the Internet, and then to cite that information in proper citation format.

Technology Skill(s): Searching the Internet, COPY and PASTE, basic e-mail.

Process:
Today's assignment is a "treasure hunt" intended to extend your ability to do research on-line. To complete the assignment, locate sites with the following information and create a works cited entry for each. Write entries in an e-mail window, a word-processing program, or on a scrap sheet of paper so you can turn them in before the end of class. To receive full credit for this assignment you must finish the first five entries; for each one you complete correctly after number 5 you will receive 1 point extra credit.

"Treasure List"
1. The Columbia site that shows you how to cite sources gathered off the Internet. (Hint: look for the name Janice Walker).
2. The Declaration of Independence
3. A review of the movie *Life is Beautiful*
4. A page that describes Netiquette
5. A page that lists links to good writing resources
6. A picture of the Statue of Liberty
7. A newsgroup posting about the Y2K problem
8. A full-text copy of Shakespeare's *Hamlet*
9. An on-line Grammar Quiz
10. An on-line chemistry journal
11. The official White House site.
12. A site devoted to Jeanette Winterson
13. A definition of a computer virus
14. A site that describes the history of the Internet
15. A recipe for oatmeal raisin cookies

Notes:
If the class has not yet gone over effective search techniques, teachers might want to include such a discussion with this assignment. A shorter version of this exercise might ask student to find the "treasure" without worrying about the citation. Teachers using this variation might discuss citation styles during a future class period.
Teachers who wish to expand this exercise could have students evaluate the Web sites that they find during this search.

Plan B:
This exercise can work well in a library, using print resources instead of electronic.

Search Engine Topic Exploration

Pedagogical Objective: This exercise asks students to find information about a topic, and then use the results of that search process as a pre-writing prompt for further exploration.

Technology Skill(s): Search, CUT and PASTE

Process:
Today, we going to be a Web search engine to help explore your paper topics. As always, please read through the entire assignment before doing anything else.

To begin, please go to <http://ww.snap.com>. Snap! is a Web search engine, but don't write your topic in the search field. Instead, find the "categories" heading located in the page. With your topic in mind, think of which category you might find your topic in, and write that category down in an e-mail window, a word processor window, or on a piece of paper.

Now click on the category you have chosen. You'll notice that you are now given a list of sub-categories. Again, find the sub-category that you think should contain your topic, and write it down. Repeat this process until you find a list of sites that concern your topic, or until you reach a dead-end.

If you hit a dead-end, retrace your steps, one at a time, until you do find your site. Note dead-ends on your path document. If you get truly stuck, please raise your hand, and I'll come over and try to give you some pointers.

When you find the sites you are looking for listed, please include the best three as potential resources for your paper. If you find that your topic is listed as a category, please indicate that as well.

Below, I've included an example of what your path might look like.

    Topic: Artificial Intelligence
    Path: Science & Technology
                  History of Science
                          DEAD END
                Computer Science
                      *Artificial Intelligence
Sites:
    • AIBrain: "Download and test AIBrain, an artificial intelligence program for Microsoft Windows." <http://www.geocities.com/CapeCanaveral/Lab/7677/index.html>.

    • Artificial Intelligence and Robotics Project: "This site describes the research being done in artificial intelligence, including knowledge representation and acquisition, machine reasoning and learning, artificial perception and intelligent automation." <http://www.elet.polimi.it/section/compeng/air/>/

• Artificial Intelligence FAQ "Here you can find the six-part series of frequently asked questions and answers about artificial intelligence." <http://www.cs.cmu.edu/Groups/AI/html/faqs/ai/ai_general/top.html>

When you are finished with your search, visit the three sites in question and read through the information.

On the same document, write down any sub-categories you find listed for your topic. A good way to find sub-categories is to look for links that narrow your topic down into specific sub-areas. In the above example, for instance, I would find that "artificial perception" is a sub-category of artificial intelligence.

After you have visited each site and made note of the sub-categories, write a paragraph explaining how you plan to focus your topic for your next paper. This paragraph can be an informal exploration of your ideas.

When you are done, please e-mail a copy of the document to me.

Notes:
Teachers can expand this lesson by asking students to write down the correct citations for each of the resources they find, or by summarizing the resource pages. Especially ambitious teachers might have this exercise lead to the development of a formal prospectus for their papers.

Teachers should feel free to use Search engines other than Snap!, but should keep in mind that the search engine needs to have a category listing such as that provided by Snap! Yahoo is an obvious alternate.

Plan B:
There is no "traditional classroom" version of this assignment, though students might be able to use the electronic card catalog of the school library to accomplish much the same thing. Instead of Web-site resources, they will find print resources. Ideally, students will use both printed and electronic resources for projects like research papers.

Web Page Credibility

Pedagogical Objective: This exercise asks students to evaluate the credibility of Web pages.

Technology Skill(s): Using the World Wide Web.

Process:

Today, we are going to be looking at how to evaluate information we find off the World Wide Web. When we find a book in the library, we tend to assume that the information contained in that book is correct. Publishers require a degree of competence by their authors, and will not publish a book by just anyone. We trust that the author and the publisher of the text are truthful and if nothing else, want to avoid the embarrassment of having thousands of printed books with incomplete or incorrect information. Once books have been printed and distributed, it is very difficult to retract or correct mistakes.

Web pages, on the other hand, can be published by anyone with access to a computer. There are few "controls" or editorial boards to review the information on Web pages before they are published, and Web pages can change in a matter of minutes. Evaluating the information we find from and source is important, but is essential for the Internet.

To begin today's assignment, go to following site and read the evaluation criteria and examples given: <http://lib.nmsu.edu/staff/susabeck/eval.html>

When you have finished, please write an evaluation (click here for an e-mail window or use a word processor) that compares BOTH of the following sites using all of the appropriate criteria:

<http://www.y2ksupplies.com/>
<http://www.mille.org/y2kpage.html>

When you are finished, please SEND the mail, or PRINT me a copy of the assignment.

Finally, for homework, find a "reliable" site related to your research topic, and using the evaluation criteria we looked at today, write a short (one page) justification of why you think the site is credible (you'll include this document in you final portfolio, so make sure you SAVE and print a copy).

Notes:
There are many sites available that discuss Internet source evaluation criteria (see Chapter 8 for some examples). One of the "lessons" of this exercise for teachers is that you do not have to make up everything yourself. Use the resources out there -- just make sure to evaluate that information yourself before using it in class!

Perhaps obviously, the two example sites concerning the Y2K issue can be replaced by sites more relevant to your course.

Plan B:
This exercise depends upon an active and working connection to the Web. Teachers who do not have such access can print out the evaluation criteria found on the page referenced, or make up their own. Reproducing the pages to evaluate is a bit harder, since the evaluation partly depends upon the nature of the links involved, but teachers could certainly use a print copy to begin a discussion about evaluation of both electronic and printed sources.

Hypertext Reading

<u>Pedagogical Objective</u>: This is an advanced writing exercise that asks students to consider the nature of hypertext (and, by implication, of linear texts) by reading three different kind of self-reflexive hypertextual works.

<u>Technology Skill(s)</u>: Basic Web browsing.

<u>Process</u>:

Today, we are going to explore the wonders of hypertext. As you know, a hypertext is a document with the ability to link to other documents. The most common examples of hypertext (besides Web pages, of course) can be found in HELP menus. See the HELP menu? Go ahead and click on it, and choose "Contents." When you read through most help topics, you'll notice that there are words you can click on that take you to related issues. That is an example of a simple hypertext.

Today we're going to look at some more innovative examples of hypertext. These examples are all texts that "push the envelope" of how hypertexts work, and all talk about the concept of hypertext even as they talk about it (and thus, are interesting examples of the relationship between form and content).

As we go through the following sites, I would like you to write a review for each (think of this exercise like you are writing a book or movie review). Include the following information:

- In what ways was this text similar to a printed book?
- In what ways was it different from a printed book?
- What was the best thing about the site?
- What was the worst thing about the site?
- What, if any, was the point of this site? What goals do you think the author(s) is (are) trying to achieve with this site? Do you think the site is successful?
- Would you recommend this site to anyone you know? Your mother? Your child? A stranger? A friend?
- Do you think the information on this site is credible? Why or why not.
- Describe your general reaction to the page.

The first example is probably going to look the most familiar, because it's an encyclopedia. And if you think about it, encyclopedia are kinds of hypertexts anyway (or at least, texts that are designed to be read in a non-linear, jump-and-go sort of way).
<http://clever.net/cam/encyclopedia.html>
The next two sites are bit more "explorative" and operate in some unusual ways.
<http://home.earthlink.net/~outlyr/hypertext/hyper.htm>
<http://web.nwe.ufl.edu/~scooper/demo.html>
And finally, here is a site that really pushes the virtual envelope. Have fun with this one!
<http://www.superbad.com>

Notes:
This exercise should not be used early in the semester, and should only be used by classes that use the Internet on a fairly regular basis, because it asks students to "explore" some of the more interesting aspects of hypertext. Though at the time this book was written, all three of these sites were up and working, teachers should obviously double-check to make sure they are still there before class.

There are many other examples of interesting hypertexts out on the Web. Teachers might want to look at the Voice of the Shuttle, under the Technology of Writing section, for more ideas and examples (<http://humanitas.ucsb.edu/>).

Teachers should also be aware that this exercise is fairly advanced, insofar as it asks students to think about the differences between print and electronic media, and to write about those differences in a "review" type format.

Plan B:
There is no "traditional classroom" equivalent to this exercise.

Appendix A

Glossary

ASCII [American Standard Code for Information Exchange] -- Basic no-frills text. ASCII documents are also referred to as "text only" documents, and usually contain only alphanumeric characters without any special formatting features, such as bold or italics.

Asynchronous discourse -- Literally, "different time" communication. The most familiar example of asynchronous discourse is traditional letter writing, where a considerable space of time elapses between one act of communication and the next. In terms of the electronic environment, asynchronous discourse usually refers to e-mail, newsgroups, or mailing lists. Though the electronic environment reduces transmission time to almost negligible quantities (e-mail takes only seconds to travel thousands of miles), asynchronous discourse is nevertheless staggered and discreet insofar as users need not reply immediately in order to be part of a conversation.

Attachments -- Attachments are files that ride piggyback upon on an e-mail message. Attachments can be very useful as they preserve the original formatting of the file in question, allowing users to share information and files directly. Attachments can also be problematic, first because they require that the recipient of the file can open (i.e., use) it on their computer, and second because files can be very large. For example, if a Microsoft Word '97 document were sent as an attachment, the recipient would need Microsoft Word '97 (or a program able to open such files accurately) in order to open the file.

Bare-bones word processor -- A streamlined word processor without many of the special features that characterize full-featured word processors. Bare-bones word processors usually come pre-installed on most personal computers, and often offer the easiest path to a writing space. Bare-bones word processors are especially important for older or slower computers that might have trouble running larger, fancier programs, or if users are doing heavy multi-tasking that results in computer delays.

BBS [Bulletin Board System] -- See *newsgroup.*

Bookmark -- A bookmark, also called a "favorites" folder or file, is a function of a Web browser that stores the location of a particular Web page for easy access later. Bookmarks allow users to jump directly to a saved location instead of navigating to that site manually. Bookmark files are normally saved as HTML files, so can be viewed or sent like any Web page.

Boolean operator -- A type of expression with two possible values: "true" and "false." The most common Boolean functions are AND, OR, and NOT. Boolean operators are used by Web-based search engines to narrow a query. For example, the search for "run AND play" will return only those pages with both terms, while "run NOT play" returns only those pages that include the term "run" but do not include the term "play."

Bounce -- E-mail messages that cannot be delivered are usually returned to the sender with an explanation of the problem. This returned message is called a bounce. Bounces often appear to be messages written from "Mailer Daemon," which is a program that handles e-mail routing.

Cache -- When users browse the Web, they are actually receiving electronic copies of those Web pages. These copies are kept in the local hard drive of the user's machine, in a special file called a cache. Caches reduce the time needed to load frequently accessed Web sites, because they store most or all of the information in local memory.

CGI [Common Gateway Interface] -- A Common Gateway Interface is a doorway for a computer program (usually written in **perl**) that functions in conjunction with Web pages. Most search engines use CGI's to collect data from the user (the search terms), perform an activity (searching through its database), and return to the user the results of the inquiry. CGI's can be used for many purposes, and require a good deal of technical expertise to create or edit.

Client-side -- A Client-side program is one that operates from a user's local machine. Client-side applications are distinguished from server-side applications, which run off a central server. E-mail programs such as Netscape Mail, Eudora, and Outlook Express, are all client-side applications.

Clipboard -- The clipboard is an invisible storage area on a personal computer. Text or data that is COPIED or CUT is stored in the clipboard until the user CLEARS the clipboard, turns off the machine, or COPIES something else. Users are able to PASTE the contents of the clipboard into any text input field, such as a word processor.

CMC [Computer-Mediated Communication] -- CMC is the updated term for CAI [Computer Assisted Instruction]. Whereas the term CAI implies a degree of stasis for educational practices (the tools may change, but the goals and basic processes remain constant), CMC recognizes the fundamental environmental and pedagogical changes implicit in the new media.

Coding -- Coding usually refers to writing HTML code manually, as opposed to using a WYSIWIG editor.

Copy -- One of the three most common and useful functions of modern computers, the COPY command takes highlighted (blocked) text or data and stores a copy of that information on the clipboard, ready to be PASTED into a destination document.

Cut -- Another of the three most common and useful functions of modern computers, the CUT command also takes highlighted (blocked) text or data and stores a copy of that information on the clipboard. Unlike COPY, however, the CUT command removes the highlighted information from the source document.

Dialogue Box -- A pop-up window that requires user interaction. The OPEN FILE dialogue box, for example, asks the user to specify the location of the file to be opened.

DOS [Disk Operating System] -- An operating system with a textual, rather than graphical, interface. The term DOS is currently used in two main ways: 1) to distinguish computers that run Macintosh software from those that do not; 2) To distinguish older (DOS-based) programs from those that are native to a Windows OS. Both uses of the term derive from the period of time before Windows95, when nearly all non-Macintosh PC's used a version of DOS.

Electronic Environment -- A term that describes the literal and virtual spaces of computer-mediated communication (CMC) as opposed to the environment of the traditional classroom environment.

E-mail -- Electronic mail. This term is used as both a verb to describe the act of composing and sending a text document across the Internet to a specified recipient, and as a noun to describe the text so sent.

Flaming -- Term used to describe annoying, harassing, or malicious e-mail messages. Due to the distancing effect of e-mail upon authority, and the speed with which e-mail messages can be composed and sent, flaming can be a serious problem. Users who flame others usually end up having their e-mail accounts suspended or worse, depending upon the nature of the transgression, because most people who flame forget they are sending little packages of evidence, complete with date and time stamp.

Forms -- On a Web page, a form is a special HTML tag that allows certain kinds of interaction with the reader of the text. Some forms can be used to submit information (to a search engine, for example), while others are used for navigation or to solicit information (for an on-line quiz or test, for example).

Frozen -- Computers that stop responding to keyboard or mouse input are called frozen. Sometimes, users with a bit of troubleshooting knowledge can correct the problem, or at least minimize it (by warm booting, for example). Other times, only the "reset" switch or the "on/off" button can resolve the situation.

FTP [File Transfer Protocol] -- Simply, FTP is used to move files electronically from one computer to another. FTP describes both the action of transferring files in this way, and the program used to transfer them.

Full-featured word-processing suite -- Word processors with all the bells and whistles, such as Microsoft Word and Corel WordPerfect. Such programs tend to be very large, and can perform an amazing range of functions.

GIF [Graphic Interchange Format] -- An image file format that can display up to 256 colors. GIF is one of the two standard graphic file types that are used in Web pages, and is the format normally used for small icons, such as bullets and banners.

Global replace -- A command found in many word processors, the global replace function allows users to replace one word or phrase with another throughout an entire document regardless of length. The COPY and PASTE keyboard shortcuts are especially useful in conjunction with GLOBAL REPLACE.

GUI [Graphical User Interface] -- An operating system that operates through use of icons and "windows." Microsoft Windows (3.1, 95, 98, NT) and MacOS are both examples of GUI operating systems.

Hit -- A term that describes a positive result from an Internet search engine.

HTML [Hypertext MarkUp Language] -- The programming language of World Wide Web documents. Nearly every Web page accessible through the Internet is written in HTML, which is currently in its fourth version. HTML codes (and therein, Web pages) are actually ASCII documents that include special phrases called "tags."

HTTP [HyperText Transfer Protocol] -- This initial portion of most URL's, "HTTP" indicates that the location should be accessed as a World Wide Web document. In general, any time users see "http" they can assume they are going to be looking at a Web page or something that can be accessed as if it were. HTTP is distinguished from other protocols, such as FTP and gopher.

Hyperlink, Hotlink, Link -- A link is a command that opens a pathway to another document or file. When users click on the link, the referent document is automatically loaded, usually into the same window. The World Wide Web is based upon the existence of linked hypertextual documents. Hypercard is an older Macintosh example of a program that works with hypertexts.

Internet -- Though sometimes mistakenly thought to be synonymous with the World Wide Web, the Internet actually encompasses a much broader spectrum of electronic resources, including e-mail, MOO's and MUD's, gopher, telnet, and more. The Internet is the global electronic environment, in all its many forms.

ISP [Internet Service Provider] -- In order for most people to connect to the Internet, they must go through an ISP to provide the Internet connection. An ISP is the Internet equivalent of a local phone company, providing users computer access to the outside world.

Java -- A programming language developed by Sun Microsystems. Java is something of a unique language, in that it supports programming for the Internet in the form of platform-independent "applets." In other words, Java mini-programs operate regardless of the operating system of the client computer, which makes them very popular for use on the Internet.

Javascript -- A programming language developed by Netscape for use with Web pages. Unlike Java "applets," Javascripts are sometimes embedded within the HTML code of a Web page. Javascripts can also operate as server-side applications.

JPEG [Joint Photographics Expert Group] -- An image file format that can display up to 16 million colors. One of the two standard graphic file types that are used in Web pages, the JPEG format tends to be used for high-resolution images, such as photographs.

Local Area Network (LAN) -- A discrete series of computers that share information through local servers. Local Area Networks are normally not accessible over the Internet, and certainly not to the general public (that would defeat the point). Many schools and businesses use LANs to create a secure computing environment in which information can be shared and stored.

Lurking -- Users who subscribe to and read newsgroups or mailing lists but do not write anything themselves are lurking. Many newsgroups suggest that new subscribers lurk for a period of time before posting, to get a feel for the nature and practices of the group's discussions.

Mass mail link-- On a Web page, a mass mail link is a single hyperlink that mails more than one person. Though there is no technical limit to the number of addresses one can include in a mass mail link, anything over 25 is obnoxious and generally frowned upon. If more than 25 people need to be mailed, newsgroups and mailing lists work well.

MOO [Multi-User Object Oriented Environment] -- Like MUDs, MOOs are electronic environments that define portions of virtual space. Unlike a MOO, MUDs can create Objects with which users can interact. For example, a student might "enter" her "virtual classroom" inside a MUD, and read the "Blackboard." Objects are like textual descriptions with certain properties, waiting to be looked at or used in order to activate.

MUD [Multi-User Dimension (or Dungeon)] -- Popularized for role-playing games, these electronic environments create virtual spaces in which participants can "speak" and "act."

Multi-tasking -- Performing more than one operation at a time. Typically, students will need to multi-task for assignments or exercises that require multiple programs operating simultaneously, such as a word processor and a Web browser. Multi-tasking is standard operating procedure for many environments, but teachers should be wary. Too much multi-tasking can cause older or slower computers to operate very slowly or freeze.

Netiquette -- Netiquette is the set of courtesy guidelines that help govern the way people communicate electronically. Netiquette sources vary radically, but the Internet community takes some guidelines, such as those concerning harrassment and "flaming," very seriously.

Newsgroup -- A newsgroup is a centralized mechanism to share information. Also called bulletin boards, users can usually both read from and post e-mail messages to public newsgroups. The print equivalent of a newsgroup would be something like an editorial page where everyone could publish an opinion whenever they wanted. Some newsgroups are restricted in such a way that users can only read messages, but these are usually used for administrative purposes.

Operating system -- An operating system, or OS, is like the root language spoken by a computer. The operating system is the software foundation of the computer, and determines the kind of application that the computer can run. The most familiar operating systems (Windows 95, Windows NT, OS/2, MacOS, and until recently DOS) are used in personal computers, while others (UNIX, LINUX, MVS, NOVELL) are usually found in mainframe systems and servers. The important element for most users to remember here is that the operating system is not an application as much as it is the environment through which applications run.

Paste -- One of the most standard computer commands, the PASTE function takes whatever the user has stored in their **clipboard** and copies it into a composition area, such as a word-processing document or e-mail composition screen. The PASTE command only works if the user has stored something in the clipboard by using COPY or CUT.

Perl [Practical Extraction and Report Language] -- A flexible programming language sometimes used on a Web server. CGI's often utilize programs written in Perl to manipulate data.

Pine [Program for Internet News & E-mail] -- PINE is a Unix-based server-side e-mail program, usually accessed through telnet. More simply, PINE is a text-only e-mail program that users must access remotely.

Plug-ins -- Plug-ins are small attachment programs that add to the functionality of a Web browser. Plug-ins are used to play sounds, display movies and animation, and perform other special multi-media functions. Plug-ins normally need to be installed manually, but are usually free.

Protocol -- One of several specific methods by which computers "talk" to one another. Hypertext Transfer Protocol (**http**) is the "grammar" of the World Wide Web.

Server -- A computer that "serves" or distributes information to other machines ("clients"). Web pages must be published on a Web server to be accessed remotely. "Server" refers to both a physical computer and the software that allows information to be distributed.

Server-side applications -- Programs that run off a remote server instead of a local hard drive. Search engines use server-side applications to find information for users (the "server" machine is the one that runs the program that searches through a database and returns "hits" to the user). In a LAN setting, it is possible that ALL applications run server-side. In such a case, users would need to log into the network in order to do anything.

Spam -- Unsolicited and unwanted e-mail, usually sent in great quantities. "Spamming" is very bad.

Synchronous discourse -- Communication that occurs in real time (literally, "same time" communication). Typically, synchronous discourse refers to the kind of exchange one finds in a MOO, MUD, or chat room. Some synchronous environments are nearly instantaneous, where users can see the message as it is being composed, but most allow the author to compose on a separate screen before sending the message to the group.

Telnet -- An Internet application that allows users to "log in" to remote computers. Typically, users "telnet" to distant servers to access e-mail, browse through resources, or download information.

Thread -- Any particular topic of discussion. Most newsgroups and mailing lists have several discussions or "threads" at any given time.

Unix, UNIX -- A flexible and programmer-friendly operating system usually used in servers. Unix is not an acronym, but both spellings are commonly accepted.

URL [Uniform Resource Locator] -- Every piece of electronic data accessible over the Internet has a URL, which is like a numeric street address. The URL identifies the computer and file path of the data, as well as the protocol or "language" needed to retrieve that data.

Virus -- A computer virus is like a weed. It is a small program that users don't want, and it tends to reproduce itself until it clutters the garden.

The term "virus" actually refers to four different kinds of "weeds": true viruses, trojan horses, worms, and bombs. A virus is a program that replicates itself in certain areas of the infected machine. A trojan horse is a program that does what it should, but carries a little something extra (such as a virus or a bomb). A worm is a program that "burrows" its way into a computers hard drive, eating random chunks of data. A bomb is a program that waits until a certain time or event, and then "blows up." Most viruses are not malevolent, but are designed to do cute or stupid little things. Users CANNOT get a virus by reading simple text e-mail: viruses are programs that must be downloaded and then executed in order to launch.

Web browser -- A software program capable of displaying HTML documents. Web browsers require an active Internet connection to display remote files.

Web page editor -- A software program that helps users create HTML pages, either through a WYSIWYG interface, semi-automated HTML code generation, or a combination of both.

Wide Area Network (WAN) -- A wide area network joins together several Local Area Networks. The Internet could be considered to be the ultimate WAN.

Word processor -- A software program designed to produce textual documents.

World Wide Web -- The series of hypertextual electronic documents interconnected through links, and the servers that distribute and execute those documents when appropriate.

WYSIWYG [What You See is What You Get] -- A document composition program (such as a word processor) in which the version of the text displayed in the editor window is more or less equivalent to the final product. Nearly all modern word processors use WYSIWYG formats.

Appendix B

Writing Basic Course Web Pages

This appendix contains an example of a course Web site. This template is a simple and effective site that is very easy for teachers to edit and use. We have included a screen shot of what the final Web page looks like, a few simple directions on how to use the template, and the HTML code that produces that pages. This appendix also includes the HTML Codes for the three Web-based lesson plans shown in Chapter 14.

Teachers should realize that there are thousands of ways to organize Web pages, and this example is offered only for convenience.

Using the Template

The best way for teachers to get and use this Web page template is to go to the on-line version, posted at <http://www.niu.edu/facdev/curriculum/choice.html>. This link will take teachers to a Web site that provides the template and detailed instructions on how to use it. Teachers should be aware that this site is customized for teachers at Northern Illinois University, but also that it is fairly easy to edit.

Alternately, teachers can write the HTML code provided below into a bare-bones word processor, exactly as written. Line breaks normally do not matter, but capitalization and punctuation sometimes make a difference. After the code has been entered, teachers should SAVE the document as an HTML file. To do this, teachers would simply select FILE, SAVE AS and add the extension ".html" to the file name.

General HTML Instructions

Every Web page is written in HTML, which is a very simple ASCII-based language. This means that anyone can write a Web page using a simple (bare-bones) word processor. Let's look at an example:

HI THERE!!

Isn't my new page groovy?

If you like it, please e-mail me at student@somewhere.net

Figure B-1: Sample Web page

This is obviously a very simple Web page. It has no pictures, but does include a hyperlinked e-mail address. Now, let's take a look at the HTML script for this page:

```html
<html>
<head>
  <meta name="Author" content="Eric Hoffman">
  <meta name="GENERATOR" content="Mozilla/4.5 [en] (WinNT; I) [Netscape]">
  <title>sample1</title>
</head>
<body>
<center>
<h1>HI THERE!!</h1></center>
<center>
<p>
<br>Isn't my new page groovy?
<p>If you like it, please e-mail me at
<a href="mailto:student@somewhere.net">student@somewhere.net</a>
</center>
</body>
</html>
```

Figure B-2: HTML source for B-1

The HTML source code may look a bit intimidating, but it is really quite simple. All of the commands contained within angle brackets are called "tags" and are instructions to the Web browser. The tag <html> tells the browser that it is reading a Web page. The tag </html> tells the browser where the end of the Web page is located (note that a forward slash "/" is used to "end" a tag). Everything contained between <head> and </head> is information contained within the "header" of the document, and is not displayed with the page itself. Everything contained between <body> and </body> is the visible portion of the Web page. The <center> and </center> tags are used to center images or lines of text. Both <p> and <br> are line breaks. The <h1> tag is used to designate a font size, in this case, very big ("H" tags are numbered from 1 to 6, in decreasing size values, so an <h1> tag is the biggest font, while <h6> is the smallest). The only other tag used in the example above is <a href>. This is the tag used to create a hyperlink. In the case above, the hyperlink is used to designate an e-mail link. The hyperlink tag has three elements: the link referent, the link signifier, and the link closure. In the example above, the first part of the tag, <a href="mailto:student@somewhere.net"> defines the link action. In this case, the "mailto" section asks the browser to open up a new e-mail window addressed to "student@somewhere.net". The second part of the link is the text that we find between the other sections. In this case, the text reads student@somewhere.net, and comprises the link signifier; that is, the actual words the user clicks in order to activate the link. There is no necessary causal relationship between the link signifier and the link referent (in other words, the signifier here could read "monkeys have tails," and when the user clicked on it, would still open a mail window pre-addressed to student@somewhere.net). The final portion of the link script, </a>, simply closes the link.

We have gone through this script at some length for two reasons. First, HTML scripts are very easy to learn. Second, HTML is easy to create. Anyone with a word processor could type in the above script, SAVE the document as an HTML document, and open it in a Web browser, and it would work fine.

Web Page Template

This template is a simple page that uses a "vertical" design. All of the information is included on the same page, and teachers can edit the page very easily using a Web editor (such as FrontPage, Netscape Composer or Adobe PageMill), or even in the HTML script using a bare-bones word processor such as Notepad.[25]

Figure B-3 shows what the empty template looks like on the Web, and Figures B-4, B-5, and B-6 contain the script for that page.

To edit this template, teachers should look for text NOT enclosed within angle brackets. Such text is actually displayed on the page itself (though is modified by surrounding tags), and can be edited like any normal text. The easiest way for teachers to complete their syllabus is to have the "normal" print syllabus open in a word-processing document, and use the COPY and PASTE functions to transfer text into the Web page. Of course, teachers can just type the text into the Web template itself in the appropriate location. Figures B-7 and B-8 illustrate the script from a Web site that has been partially filled out, and Figures B-9 and B-10 show what the completed page might look like.

---

[25] Note that users working directly with HTML script should use a bare-bones word processor such as Notepad or Simpletext. Full-featured word-processors tend to add extra "coding" to the documents that prevents them from working correctly.

Blank Template

School Name/Graphic

Department Name

Course Name/Number/Section
Semester

- **Professor**
- **Texts**
- **Assignments**
- **Reading List**

- **E-Mail Address**
- **Course Requirements**
- **Links**
- **Course Newsgroup**

- **Course Description**
- **Additional Information**
- **Department Page**

Course/Section

Professor:
Meeting time and place:
Office address/phone:
Home phone: (OPTIONAL)
Office hours:
E-Mail:***
***[Supply statement detailing reasonable use of e-mail by students, including a time frame specifying how long students can expect to wait for a response from the instructor.]
- **Return to top of page**

Course description/objectives:
Required/recommended texts:
Course requirements:
Grading:
Attendance policy:
Plagiarism Statement:"The attempt of any student to present as his or her own work that which he or she has not produced is regarded by the faculty and administration as a serious offense. Students are considered to have cheated if they copy the work of another during an examination or turn in a paper or an assignment written, in whole or in part, by someone else. Students are guilty of plagiarism, intentional or not, if they copy material from books, magazines, or other sources or if they paraphrase ideas from such sources without acknowledging them. Students guilty of, or assisting others in, either cheating or plagiarism on an assignment, quiz, or examination may receive a grade of F for the course involved and may be suspended or dismissed from the university." *Northern Illinois University Undergraduate Catalog*.
Additional Information:
Reading List:

Figure B-3: Blank Template

HTML Script for the Blank Template

```html
<!doctype html public "-//w3c//dtd html 4.0 transitional//en">
<html>
<head>
  <meta http-equiv="Content-Type" content="text/html; charset=iso-8859-1">
  <meta name="GENERATOR" content="Mozilla/4.5 [en] (WinNT; I) [Netscape]">
  <title>Faculty Course-Page Template</title>
</head>
<body text="#000000" bgcolor="#FFFFFF" link="#478D8D" vlink="#551A8B" alink="#FF0000"
background="graytext.gif">

<center>
<h2>
<i>School Name</i><a NAME="top"></a></h2></center>

<center><b><i><font size=+3>Department Name</font></i></b>
<p><img SRC="teal.jpg" height=5 width=620>
<p><b><i><font size=+1>Course Name/Number/Section</font></i></b>
<br><b>Semester</b></center>

<br> 
<br> 
<center><table CELLSPACING=0 CELLPADDING=0 >
<tr>
<td WIDTH="225" HEIGHT="20"><img SRC="tealball.gif" height=14 width=14><b>
<a href="#professor">Professor</a></b></td>

<td WIDTH="225" HEIGHT="20"><img SRC="tealball.gif" height=14 width=14><b>
<a href="mailto:carols@niu.edu">E-Mail
Address</a></b></td>

<td WIDTH="225" HEIGHT="20"><img SRC="tealball.gif" height=14 width=14><b>
<a href="#course">Course
Description</a></b></td>
</tr>

<tr>
<td WIDTH="225" HEIGHT="20"><img SRC="tealball.gif" height=14 width=14><b>
<a href="#texts">Texts</a></b></td>

<td WIDTH="225" HEIGHT="20"><img SRC="tealball.gif" height=14 width=14><b>
<a href="#Requirements">Course
Requirements</a></b></td>

<td WIDTH="225" HEIGHT="20"><img SRC="tealball.gif" height=14 width=14><b>
<a href="#info">Additional
Information</a></b></td>
</tr>

<tr>
<td><img SRC="tealball.gif" height=14 width=14>  <b><a
href="http://www.niu.edu/facdev/curriculum/spring99.html">Assignments</a></b></td>

<td><img SRC="tealball.gif" height=14 width=14><b> <a href="#Links">Links</a></b></td>
```

Figure B-4: HTML Script for the Blank Template

```
<td><img SRC="tealball.gif" height=14 width=14><b> <a
href="http://www.niu.edu/facdev/curriculum">Department
Page</a></b></td>
</tr>

<tr>
<td><img SRC="tealball.gif" height=14 width=14><b> <a href="#reading">Reading
List</a></b></td>

<td><img SRC="tealball.gif" height=14 width=14><b> <a href="news://news.niu.edu/...">Course
Newsgroup</a></b></td>

<td></td>
</tr>

<tr>
<td WIDTH="225" HEIGHT="20"></td>

<td WIDTH="225" HEIGHT="20"></td>

<td WIDTH="225" HEIGHT="20"></td>
</tr>
</table></center>

<center><img SRC="teal.jpg" height=5 width=620>
<br><b>Course/Section</b></center>

<p><a NAME="professor"></a><b>Professor</b>:
<p><b>Meeting time and place</b>:
<p><b>Office address/phone</b>:
<p><b>Home phone</b>:   (<b>OPTIONAL</b>)
<p><b>Office hours</b>:
<p><b><a href="mailto:professor@niu.edu">E-Mail</a>:</b>***
<p>***[Supply statement detailing reasonable use of e-mail by students,
including a time frame specifying how long students can expect to wait
for a response from the instructor.]
<p><img SRC="tri_lb.gif" height=10 width=20><b><a href="#top">Return to
top of page</a></b>
<br> 
<p><br>
<br>
<center>
<p><img SRC="teal.jpg" height=5 width=620></center>

<p><a NAME="course"></a><b>Course description/objectives</b>:
<p><a NAME="texts"></a><b>Required/recommended texts</b>:
<p><a NAME="Requirements"></a><b>Course requirements</b>:
<p><a NAME="Grading"></a><b>Grading</b>:
<p><a NAME="Attendance"></a><b>Attendance policy</b>:
<p><a NAME="Plagiarism"></a><b>Plagiarism Statement</b>:"The attempt of
any student to present as his or her own work that which he or she has
not produced is regarded by the faculty and administration as a serious
offense. Students are considered to have cheated if they copy the work
of another during an examination or turn in a paper or an assignment written,
in whole or in part, by someone else. Students are guilty of plagiarism,
intentional or not, if they copy material from books, magazines, or other
```

Figure B-5: HTML Script for the Blank Template (continued)

sources or if they paraphrase ideas from such sources without acknowledging them. Students guilty of, or assisting others in, either cheating or plagiarism on an assignment, quiz, or examination may receive a grade of F for the course involved and may be suspended or dismissed from the university."
<i>Northern
Illinois University Undergraduate Catalog</i>.
<p><a NAME="info"></a><b>Additional Information</b>:
<p><a NAME="reading"></a><b>Reading List</b>:
<p><img SRC="tri_lb.gif" height=10 width=20><b><a href="#top">Return to top of page</a></b>

<center>
<p><img SRC="teal.jpg" height=5 width=620>

<a NAME="Links"></a><b>LINKS to Relevant Academic Sites:</b></center>

<p><b><a href="http://www.niu.edu/facdev/curriculum/citing.html">Electronic Citation Style Manuals</a></b>
<p><b><a href="http://www.niu.edu/facdev/curriculum/evaluate.htm">Evaluating Internet Sources</a></b>

<p>

<center>
<p><img SRC="teal.jpg" height=5 width=620></center>

<p><img SRC="tri_lb.gif" height=10 width=20><b><a href="#top">Return to top of page</a></b>
<p><img SRC="tri_lb.gif" height=10 width=20><b><a href="http://www.niu.edu/facdev">Return to [department] homepage</a></b>
<p><img SRC="tri_lb.gif" height=10 width=20><b><a href="http://www.niu.edu">Return to NIU homepage</a></b>
</body>
</html>

Figure B-6: HTML Script for the Blank Template (continued)

Partially Filled-out Web script

(The area viewed here is from Figure B-5, indicated by a large side bracket.)

```
<p><a NAME="professor"></a><b>Professor</b>: Dr. Carol Scheidenhelm
<p><b>Meeting time and place</b>: MWF 8:00-8:50 Reavis Hall 301
<p><b>Office address/phone</b>: Gilbert 315;  555-2690
<p><b>Office hours</b>: I am on campus five days a week; call, e-mail,
or stop after class to make an appointment.
<p><b><a href="mailto:carols@niu.edu">E-Mail</a>:
[<a href="mailto:carols@niu.edu">carols@niu.edu</a>]
Please note:</b> Students are encouraged to e-mail me with questions and
concerns about the course. I will attempt to answer all messages within
24 hours on weekdays and 48 hours on weekends.
<p><img SRC="tri_red.gif" height=10 width=20><b><a href="#top">Return to
top of page</a></b>
<center>
<p><img SRC="thmarb.jpg" height=5 width=620></center>

<p><a NAME="course"></a><b>Course description</b>: English 110 Section
9 provides students with an introduction to short fiction and novels as
a study of historical, social, and cultural values. The course focuses
on close, critical reading of the assigned texts and will require students
to articulate--orally in class discussion, electronically in newsgroup
discussion, and in several formal papers--their understanding of the readings.
The class will meet in a computer lab sporadically throughout the semester
to more fully explore topics introduced in class discussion.
<p><a NAME="texts"></a><b>Required texts</b>: Please be certain to buy
only the editions listed.
<br>Ellison, Ralph. <i>Invisible Man. </i>New York: Vintage. Second Vintage
International Edition, March 1995.
<br>Mizener, Arthur, Ed. <i>Modern Short Stories: The Uses of Imagination.
</i>4th.
edition. New York: WW Norton.
<br>Morrison, Toni. <i>Beloved</i>. New York: Penguin (Plume).
<br>Welty, Eudora. <i>The Optimist's Daughter</i>. New York: Vintage.
<p><a NAME="reserve"></a><b>Electronic Reserve</b>: Additional materials
will be placed on electronic reserve, which will be available by the third
week of the term.
<br> 
<p><a NAME="Requirements"></a><b>Course requirements</b>:
<ul>
<li>10% Electronic Newsgroup</li>
<li>15% Quizzes</li>
<li>15% Midterm Exam</li>
<li>20% Paper ONE</li>
<li>20% Paper TWO</li>
<li>20% Final Exam</li>
</ul>
<b>Electronic Newsgroup</b>: Class members will participate in an electronic
discussion of topics assigned by the professor and suggested by course
participants. <a href="http://www.niu.edu/~c90cls1/curriculum/news110.htm">Instruction</a>
will be provided on how to participate and on the level of participation
expected.
<p><b>Group Presentations</b>: Each student will contribute to a group
```

Figure B-7: Partially Filled-out Web script

presentation on a chosen story or novel. Presentations will count for two
quiz grades. Details can be found at
<a href="http://www.niu.edu/~c90cls1/curriculum/99virtual.htm">Virtual
Groups</a>, a page that will be updated when groups are chosen.
<p>Short Papers: Each student will write two short (4-5 page) papers
during the course of the semester. A handout and more specific information
will be provided.
<p>Quizzes: Unannounced quizzes on assigned material will be sporadically
given. Quizzes cannot be made up, so although there is not a specific attendance
requirement, not attending will jeopardize your grade.
<p><a NAME="Grading"></a>Grading:
<ul>
<li>A 90-100</li>
<li>B 80-89</li>
<li>C 70-79</li>
<li>D 60-69</li>
</ul>
<a NAME="Plagiarism"></a>Plagiarism Statement: "The attempt of any
student to present as his or her own work that which he or she has not
produced is regarded by the faculty and administration as a serious offense.
Students are considered to have cheated if they copy the work of another
during an examination or turn in a paper or an assignment written, in whole
or in part, by someone else. Students are guilty of plagiarism, intentional
or not, if they copy material from books, magazines, or other sources or
if they paraphrase ideas from such sources without acknowledging them.
Students guilty of, or assisting others in, either cheating or plagiarism
on an assignment, quiz, or examination may receive a grade of F for the
course involved and may be suspended or dismissed from the university."

Figure B-8: Partially Filled-out Web script (continued)

Completed Web Page

Department of English

English 110 Section 9
Spring 1999

- **Professor**
- **Texts**
- **Assignments**
- **Electronic Reserve**

- **E-Mail Address**
- **Course Requirements**
- **Links**
- **Handouts**

- **Course Description**
- **Course Newsgroup**
- **Department Page**
- **Virtual Groups**

English 110 Section 9
Professor: Dr. Carol Scheidenhelm
Meeting time and place: MWF 8:00-8:50 Reavis Hall 301
Office address/phone: Gilbert 315; 555-2690
Office hours: I am on campus five days a week; call, e-mail, or stop after class to make an appointment.
E-Mail:[carols@niu.edu] Please note: Students are encouraged to e-mail me with questions and concerns about the course. I will attempt to answer all messages within 24 hours on weekdays and 48 hours on weekends.

Return to top of page

Course description: English 110 Section 9 provides students with an introduction to short fiction and novels as a study of historical, social, and cultural values. The course focuses on close, critical reading of the assigned texts and will require students to articulate--orally in class discussion, electronically in newsgroup discussion, and in several formal papers--their understanding of the readings. The class will meet in a computer lab sporadically throughout the semester to more fully explore topics introduced in class discussion.
Required texts: Please be certain to buy only the editions listed.
Ellison, Ralph. *Invisible Man*. New York: Vintage. Second Vintage International Edition, March 1995.
Mizener, Arthur, Ed. *Modern Short Stories: The Uses of Imagination*. 4th. edition. New York: WW Norton.
Morrison, Toni. *Beloved*. New York: Penguin (Plume).
Welty, Eudora. *The Optimist's Daughter*. New York: Vintage.
Electronic Reserve: Additional materials will be placed on electronic reserve, which will be available by the third week of the term.

Figure B-9: Completed Web Page

Course requirements:
- 10% Electronic Newsgroup
- 15% Quizzes
- 15% Midterm Exam
- 20% Paper ONE
    - 20% Paper TWO
    - 20% Final Exam

Electronic Newsgroup: Class members will participate in an electronic discussion of topics assigned by the professor and suggested by course participants. <u>Instruction</u> will be provided on how to participate and on the level of participation expected.

Group Presentations: Each student will contribute to a group presentation on a chosen story or novel. Presentations will count for two quiz grades. Details can be found at <u>Virtual Groups</u>, a page that will be updated when groups are chosen.

Short Papers: Each student will write two short (4-5 page) papers during the course of the semester. A handout and more specific information will be provided.

Quizzes: Unannounced quizzes on assigned material will be sporadically given. Quizzes cannot be made up, so although there is not a specific attendance requirement, *not* attending will jeopardize your grade.

Grading:
- A 90-100
- B 80-89
- C 70-79
- D 60-69

Plagiarism Statement: "The attempt of any student to present as his or her own work that which he or she has not produced is regarded by the faculty and administration as a serious offense. Students are considered to have cheated if they copy the work of another during an examination or turn in a paper or an assignment written, in whole or in part, by someone else. Students are guilty of plagiarism, intentional or not, if they copy material from books, magazines, or other sources or if they paraphrase ideas from such sources without acknowledging them. Students guilty of, or assisting others in, either cheating or plagiarism on an assignment, quiz, or examination may receive a grade of F for the course involved and may be suspended or dismissed from the university." *Northern Illinois University Undergraduate Catalog.*

☞ <u>Return to top of page</u>

LINKS to Relevant Academic Sites:

<u>Electronic Citation Style Manuals</u>
<u>Evaluating Internet Sources</u>

☞ <u>Return to top of page</u>
☞ <u>Return to Department of English homepage</u>
☞ <u>Return to NIU homepage</u>

Figure B-10: Completed Web Page (continued)

HTML Sources for Lesson Plans Included in Chapter 14

Diagnostic Exercise (version 1)

```
<!DOCTYPE HTML PUBLIC "-//W3C//DTD HTML 4.0 Transitional//EN">
<HTML>
<HEAD>
  <META HTTP-EQUIV="Content-Type" CONTENT="text/html; charset=iso-8859-1">
  <META NAME="Author" CONTENT="Eric Hoffman">
  <META NAME="GENERATOR" CONTENT="Mozilla/4.06 [en] (Win95; I) [Netscape]">
  <TITLE>diagnostic1</TITLE>
</HEAD>
<BODY>

<CENTER>
<H3>
Diagnostic Exercise</H3></CENTER>
<IMG SRC="book0a.gif" HEIGHT=32 WIDTH=32>
Congratulations and welcome! Since you are obviously reading this page, you have successfully found our class Web site. This portion of our Web site will normally contain the assignment for the day, so make sure you check it as soon as you get into class. (In fact, you may want to BOOKMARK the page).

<P>Today's assignment is going to be a simple writing activity in which you tell me something about your familiarity with computers. Please follow the directions below, and raise your hand if you have any questions.
<BR>
<P>Assignment:
<BR>Before you do anything, please read through the entire assignment. You'll get lost if you start the assignment without reading all the directions first.

<P>1. <A HREF="mailto:">CLICK HERE</A>
<BR>2. In the text window below, write a paragraph that describes the kind
of experience you have using computers. Please include the following information:
<UL>
<LI>Your actual name (as it appears on my class roster).</LI>
<LI>Your preferred e-mail address.</LI>
<LI>Which word processor you normally use to write papers.</LI>
<LI>How often you use e-mail and to whom you normally write.</LI>
<LI>Your experience using the World Wide Web (even if this is it!).</LI>
<LI>What kind of computer system you normally use.</LI>
<LI>What you normally use the computer for (writing papers, e-mail, Web, games, etc.).</LI>
<LI>How you would rate yourself as a computer user (Luddite, novice, casual user, experienced user, geek, guru).</LI>
</UL>
4. When you are finished, please read over the paragraph you have written,
and proofread it carefully for spelling and punctuation errors.
<BR>5. Finally, SEND the document.
</BODY>
</HTML>
```

Figure B-11: Diagnostic Exercise (version 1) Script

Diagnostic Exercise (version 2)

```
<!DOCTYPE HTML PUBLIC "-//W3C//DTD HTML 4.0 Transitional//EN">
<HTML>
<HEAD>
  <META HTTP-EQUIV="Content-Type" CONTENT="text/html; charset=iso-8859-1">
  <META NAME="Author" CONTENT="Eric Hoffman">
  <META NAME="GENERATOR" CONTENT="Mozilla/4.06 [en] (Win95; I) [Netscape]">
  <TITLE>diagnostic2</TITLE>
</HEAD>
<BODY>

<CENTER>
<H3>
Diagnostic Exercise</H3></CENTER>
<IMG SRC="book0a.gif" HEIGHT=32 WIDTH=32> Congratulations and welcome!
Since you are obviously reading this page, you have successfully found
our class Web site. This portion of our Web site will normally contain
the assignment for the day, so make sure you check it as soon as you get
into class. (In fact, you may want to BOOKMARK the page).
<P>Today's assignment is going to be a simple writing activity in which
you tell me something about your familiarity with computers. Please follow the directions below, and
raise your hand if you have any questions.
<BR> 
<P>Assignment:
<BR>Before you do anything, please read through the entire assignment.
You'll get lost if you start the assignment without reading all the directions first.
<P>1. <A HREF="mailto:">CLICK HERE</A>
<BR>2. In the text window below, write a paragraph that describes the kind
of experience you have using computers. Please include the following information:
<UL>
<LI>Your actual name (as it appears on my class roster).</LI>
<LI>Your preferred e-mail address.</LI>
<LI>Which word processor you normally use to write papers.</LI>
<LI>How often you use e-mail and to whom you normally write.</LI>
<LI>Your experience using the World Wide Web (even if this is it!).</LI>
<LI>What kind of computer system you normally use.</LI>
<LI>What you normally use the computer for (writing papers, e-mail, Web, games,
etc.).</LI>
<LI>How you would rate yourself as a computer user (Luddite, novice, casual
user, experienced user, geek, guru).</LI>
</UL>
4. When you are finished, please read over the paragraph you have written, and proofread it carefully
for spelling and punctuation errors.
<BR>5. Finally, SEND the document.
<BR>
<P><FORM METHOD="POST" ACTION="mailto:nwr@niu.edu" enctype="text/plain">
<CENTER><TABLE BORDER=0 COLS=2 WIDTH="50%" >
<TR>
<TD>Your Name:</TD>
```

Figure B-12: Diagnostic Exercise (version 2) Script

```
<TD><INPUT TYPE="text" NAME="name" SIZE="30"></TD>
</TR>
<TR>
<TD>Your preferred e-mail address:</TD>
<TD><INPUT TYPE="text" NAME="e-mail" SIZE="30"></TD>
</TR>
</TABLE></CENTER>
<CENTER>
<P>Write your assignment below:
<BR><TEXTAREA NAME="Diagnostic Exercise1" ROWS=6 COLS=40></TEXTAREA>
<P><INPUT TYPE="submit" value="SEND"><INPUT TYPE="reset"></FORM></CENTER>
</BODY>
</HTML>
```

Figure B-13: Diagnostic Exercise (version 2) Script (continued)

Final Exam

```
<!DOCTYPE HTML PUBLIC "-//W3C//DTD HTML 4.0 Transitional//EN">
<HTML>
<HEAD>
  <META HTTP-EQUIV="Content-Type" CONTENT="text/html; charset=iso-8859-1">
  <META NAME="Author" CONTENT="NWR -- Eric Hoffman">
  <META NAME="GENERATOR" CONTENT="Mozilla/4.06 [en] (Win95; I) [Netscape]">
  <TITLE>contact</TITLE>
</HEAD>
<BODY>

<CENTER>
<H1>
Final Exam</H1></CENTER>
<FORM METHOD="POST" ACTION="mailto:nwr@niu.edu" enctype="text/plain">
<BR> 
<CENTER><TABLE BORDER=0 COLS=2 WIDTH="50%" >
<TR>
<TD>Your Name:</TD>

<TD><INPUT TYPE="text" NAME="name" SIZE="30"></TD>
</TR>
</TABLE></CENTER>

<P>Instructions:
<BR>This exam is a take-home final. You should proofread your exam before handing it in (if I see a lot of stupid spelling or grammar errors, I will deduct points from your essay). You must complete this exam on your own -- you may not collaborate with another student. You may go to the writing center if you want help proofreading the document.
<P>Please read through ALL of the questions carefully. You MUST answer
question #1. Choose any TWO of the other questions, and answer them. Your answers should be as complete as possible, and should use specific examples from the texts whenever possible.

<P>Questions:
<P>
```

Figure B-14: Final Exam Script

<B>1. Based on the texts we have read and the discussions we have had in class, how would you define satire? What are its defining elements? (In other words, how can you tell if something is a satire?)</B>
<P><TEXTAREA NAME="Question#1 1. Based on the texts we have read and the discussions we have had in class, how would you define satire? What are its defining elements? (In other words, how can you tell if something is a satire?)" rows=6 cols=85 wrap="hard"></TEXTAREA>

<P>2. While discussing Monty Python's The Holy Grail, I suggested that the whole movie is summarized in the opening credits. What led me to make this claim? Do you agree with this statement or not? Support your position with tons of examples and details.
<P><TEXTAREA NAME="#2 2. While discussing Monty Python's The Holy Grail, I suggested that the whole movie is summarized in the opening credits. What led me to make this claim? Do you agree with this statement or not? Support your position with tons of examples and details." rows=6 cols=85 wrap="hard"></TEXTAREA>

<P>3. What is the purpose of satire? Or, what are some of the purposes of satire? Support your answer by considering and explaining the specific goals and methods of at least three different satires we have read this semester.
<P><TEXTAREA NAME="3. What is the purpose of satire? Or, what are some of the purposes of satire? Support your answer by considering and explaining the specific goals and methods of at least three different satires we have read this semester." rows=6 cols=85 wrap="hard"></TEXTAREA>

<P>4. Compare Gulliver as narrator (from Gulliver's Travels) to Jack as Narrator (from Stinky Cheese Man). How do they function as narrators? How do these functions relate to the satire of the text? Do these functions change through the course of the text, or do their narrative functions remain consistent? How does this change, or lack thereof, relate to the vehicle of the satire?
<P><TEXTAREA NAME="4. Compare Gulliver as narrator (from Gulliver's Travels) to Jack as Narrator (from Stinky Cheese Man). How do they function as narrators? How do these functions relate to the satire of the text? Do these functions change through the course of the text, or do their narrative functions remain consistent? How does this change, or lack thereof, relate to the vehicle of the satire?l" rows=6 cols=85 wrap="hard"></TEXTAREA>
<P>5. Compare South Park and Alice in Wonderland. Both comment on "Childhood" in some ways, and both react against what they perceive to be a stifling cultural environment. What are these "environments" that the satire reacts against? How does each text manipulate that environment? How would you identify the goal of each satire? Why are these texts read so differently today?
<P><TEXTAREA NAME="5. Compare South Park and Alice in Wonderland. Both comment on "Childhood" in some ways, and both react against what they perceive to be a stifling cultural environment. What are these "environments" that the satire reacts against? How does each text manipulate that environment? How would you identify the goal of each satire? Why are these texts read so differently today?" rows=6 cols=85 wrap="hard"></TEXTAREA>
<P>6. Compare the use of vehicle in Monty Python's The Holy Grail and Stinky Cheese Man. (Be specific).
<P><TEXTAREA NAME="6. Compare the use of vehicle in Monty Python's The Holy Grail and Stinky Cheese Man. (Be specific)." rows=6 cols=85 wrap="hard"></TEXTAREA>

<P>7. Do you think satire serves the same purpose today as it did 200 years ago? Compare the older texts we read (Swift and Carroll) with the newer texts (Stinky Cheese Man, Monty Python, South Park, I'm gonna get you sucka), and consider the different purposes and deployments of each. How are these purposes similar or different? Does satire have a future?

<P><TEXTAREA NAME="7. Do you think satire serves the same purpose today as it did 200 years ago? Compare the older texts we read (Swift and Carroll) with the newer texts (Stinky Cheese Man, Monty Python, South Park, I'm gonna get you sucka), and consider the different purposes and deployments of each. How are these purposes similar or different? Does satire have a future?" rows=6 cols=85 wrap="hard"></TEXTAREA>

Figure B-15: Final Exam Script (continued)

```
<P>8. Many of the satires we have read this semester involve the ability of language to communicate
effectively. Choose three examples, and explain how these texts satirize language, and why.
<P><TEXTAREA NAME="8. Many of the satires we have read this semester involve the ability of
language to communicate effectively. Choose three examples, and explain how these texts satirize
language, and why." rows=6 cols=85 wrap="hard"></TEXTAREA>

<P>9. Several of the satires we have read question cultural assumptions, stereotypes and myths. Pick
one such assumption, stereotype or myth, and compare its satirical treatment in at least three of the
texts we have read in class.
<P><TEXTAREA NAME="9. Several of the satires we have read question cultural assumptions,
stereotypes and myths. Pick one such assumption,
stereotype or myth, and compare its satirical treatment in at least three of the texts we have read in
class." rows=6 cols=85 wrap="hard"></TEXTAREA>

<P>EXTRA CREDIT
<BR>What is your quest?
<P><TEXTAREA NAME="EXTRA CREDIT: What is your quest?" rows=6 cols=85
wrap="hard"></TEXTAREA>
<BR>
<BR>
<CENTER>
<P>When you are finished, hit the "submit" button. Remember to proofread
your work first:
<P><INPUT TYPE="submit" value="Submit Final"><INPUT
TYPE="reset"></FORM></CENTER>

<BR> 
<P><BR>

</BODY>
</HTML>
```

Figure B-16: Final Exam Script (continued)

For those of you wondering why each of the questions is repeated in the above script, it is so that when the students send their answers, the questions are attached to the answer sheet (and thus, the questions are a bit easier to grade because the teacher knows which questions the students are trying to answer). In the script above, the first iteration of the question is the one displayed in the browser, while the copy contained within the <TEXTAREA NAME="> and </TEXTAREA> tags are included in the answers sent by the students.

Appendix C

Netiquette, Emoticons and Acronyms

Netiquette

Netiquette is Internet etiquette, and describes conventions of polite behavior. There are many pages that are devoted to describing Netiquette, but here are some of the basics:

1. No "Spamming." Spamming is the act of sending out mass unsolicited e-mail messages, usually as a form of advertising. Some companies sell lists of e-mail addresses to marketing firms, and some unscrupulous persons take advantage of this by bambarding users with unwanted e-mail messages (often advertising sites of an "adult" nature). "Spamming" is a big no-no, and most Internet Service Providers (ISPs) will revoke the account of anyone caught doing it.

2. Give credit where credit is due. As with printed documents, original information and artistic works that are posted on the Internet are protected under copyright laws. Users should not plagiarize electronic resources any more than they should plagiarize print sources.

3. Do not use or distribute pirated software. Similar to the plagiarism rule, software is protected by copyright laws, and users should comply with these rules. The most common cases of violation here concern SHAREWARE -- programs that are free for a period of time. After that period, users who wish to continue to use the program normally have to register the software and pay a nominal fee for its use. Again, this is a case of compensation. Programs (like original texts or artwork) often take a very

long time to create, and the author of the program deserves some form of compensation for the effort involved.

4. Do not Flame. A "Flame" is a deliberately antagonistic or malicious message to someone. Flames are considered extremely bad form, and on many campuses, grounds for academic discipline.

5. DO NOT USE ALL CAPS. In an e-mail message, the use of ALL CAPS is the equivalent of shouting an entire oral report.

6. Do not forward personal e-mail messages without the permission of the author. Though we normally do not think about it, an e-mail message is a copyrighted document, and as such, requires the permission of the author in order to be copied, reproduced, or re-distributed.

7. "Lurk before you Leap." When users first join a newsgroup or mailing list, it is customary to "lurk" (that is, read messages without posting) for a week or two, and read the FAQ if one exists. This custom is designed to help new users get a feel of the forum before they actively participate, and helps prevent the same discussions from being brought up every time a new user joins the group. Users who are away from a group for an extended period of time should also lurk for a while before diving back in, for the same reasons.

8. Use the Subject Line in e-mail messages. Users who receive a lot of e-mail rely upon the subject line to get a general idea of the content of the message before reading it (some users get well over 100 e-mail messages a day). Users should use the subject line to represent honestly the content of the message to help the recipient decide whether or not it's worth reading.

9. Perhaps obviously, DO NOT SEND VIRUSES to anyone!! Viruses are evil and bad.

10. Be nice to newbies. Though an unwritten rule, most Netizens try to help people who are new to the Internet community.

11. Do not send ridiculously large attachments. Attachments larger than 100K or so tend to clog up people's e-mail accounts, and take up a lot of bandwidth. If users really need to transfer large files, they should use FTP rather than e-mail.

12. Be careful with humor and sarcasm. E-mail messages can be very funny, but authors should be very careful about letting the audience know that they are joking.

13. E-mail chain letters are even worse than their print counterparts, because they can be distributed so easily and quickly. Do not send a chain letter, and if you receive one, delete it immediately (if you delete it within a minute, you won't get bad luck, whatever the letter says).

Emoticons and Acronyms

Emoticons are little symbols produced with normal ASCII characters. The most famous emoticon is the smiley, which is written :) or :-). Emoticons are viewed sideways (tilt your head to the left).

Acronyms are just what they sound like, but in terms of Internet use, refer to a set of common acronyms normally used in e-mail or synchronous environments such as Chat rooms and MOO's.

Here is a VERY basic list of emoticons and acronyms (there are thousands of each):

:-)	Smiley face	TTFN	Ta Ta For Now
:-(	Frowny Face	AFK	Away From Keyboard
:-0	Surprise	LOL	Lots Of Laughs (disbelief)
;-)	Smiley face winking	[G] or *G*	Grin (joking)
>:-(	Angry face	CYA	See ya
>:-)	Evil (mischeivous) face	L8R	Later
<:-)	Smiley face with pointy hat	ROTFL	Rolling On The Floor Laughing
:-P	Tongue sticking out	IMHO	In My Humble Opinion
:-D	Laughter	FAQ	Frequently Asked Questions
		BTW	By The Way
		FYI	For Your Information

Here are some other resources concerning Netiquette, Emoticons, and Acronyms:

- <http://www.webfoot.com/advice/email.top.html> -- A Beginner's Guide to Effective E-mail
- <http://www.fau.edu/netiquette/netiquette.html> -- Netiquette Home Page
- <http://www.jamaicans.com/online/index.htm> -- A guide to net etiquette Internet with a list common Internet acronyms, emoticons, smileys and netiquette do's and don'ts .

Appendix D

Troubleshooting Guides

Included in this appendix are basic troubleshooting guides for word processing, e-mail, and using the World Wide Web. Overall, users should remember two pieces of advice before anything else: 1) Look in the HELP menu; and 2) Report the problem to the local technical support staff. Looking in the help menu of the application in question can solve most problems, and if it cannot, then the technical support staff needs to know about the situation immediately. Technicians cannot fix things that they do not know are broken.

Basic Word-Processing Troubleshooting

Student problems with word-processing programs usually fall into three main categories: opening files, saving and printing files, and performing some specific action in a word processor.

The last of these problems is the easiest to discuss, so we shall deal with it first. If a student (or a teacher, for that matter) is having problems performing any specific actions in a word processor, the best and easiest way to solve that problem is to look through the "Index" portion of the HELP screen and find the correct procedure for performing that action.

If users cannot find the answer to the question, or if they know how to perform the action and are following the directions correctly, then they should contact their local technical support staff. The program itself may be configured in a special way, or may even need to be reinstalled to correct the problem.

Opening Files

Problem	Solution
I can't see my file.	1. The file is located elsewhere. In the OPEN FILE dialogue screen, check other folders or drives for the file. Alternately, do a Search/Find for the file. Remember to check different drives if necessary. 2. The file is saved as a different file type. In the OPEN FILE dialogue screen, check where it specifies the kind of file you are trying to open. Change this value to "All Files."
I can see my file, but it won't open.	1. Your disk may be LOCKED. Unlock it by taking the disk out of the drive, and switching the tab to the open position. 2. You may already have the file open. Check your open files. 3. Your file may be saved in a different or unreadable format. Try to open the file in a different word processor. 4. If you are double-clicking on the file itself to open it, try opening the file from within a word processor. In this case, open the file from a full-featured program if you can.
I can see and open my file, but all I get is a bunch of gibberish characters.	This is a file translation problem. 1. If you are double-clicking on the file itself to open it, try opening the file from within a word processor (this loads the file translators embedded within the word processor). In this case, open the file from a full-featured program if you can. 2. Your file may be saved in a different or unreadable format. Try to open the file from within a different word processor. 3. If neither of these work, then you will have to SAVE AS your document as a different file type, and try again. **NOTE**: NEVER try to change a file type by manually changing the document extension. This will only create a corrupt and unreadable file.
Disk error (unrecoverable disk error).	You have a bad floppy disk. Ask your lab administrator about recovering files on the damaged floppy disk. Pray.

Saving and Printing Files

Problem	Solution
The SAVE option is grayed out (inaccessible).	This version of the file is already saved. If you wish to save a copy of the file, choose SAVE AS and change the name by at least one character.
Permission denied.	1. You are trying to save to a locked disk. If you are trying to save to a floppy disk, unlock it by taking the disk out of the drive, and switching the tab to the open position. If you are trying to save to any other kind of drive (local, network), contact your lab administrator and ask about drive access. 2. You are trying to SAVE changes to a Read-only document. Choose the SAVE AS option, and change the file name.
Disk error (unrecoverable disk error).	You have a bad floppy disk. Use a different floppy. (Ask your lab administrator about recovering files on the damaged floppy disk).
I can't print.	1. Your computer is not hooked up to a printer, or the drivers are not installed -- ask your lab administrator about printing. 2. The printer requires a network password, which you have not supplied, or your network password does not allow you to print onto the network printer. Contact the lab staff for assistance. 3. You are printing to a different printer. Check the other printers in the lab for your file. If you still can't find your documents, ask your lab administrator.

E-mail Troubleshooting

In general, there are two kinds of things that can go wrong with e-mail: sending and receiving.

Sending

There are two locations where problems can occur when sending an e-mail: the sender and the recipient. If the e-mail cannot be sent at all, then the problem probably resides in the sender's location. Sometimes, the problem is simply with one of the e-mail settings that the user must fill out. More specifically, if users cannot send an e-mail message, then the problem is probably related to the OUTGOING MAIL SERVER setting. Of course, users must be connected to the Internet in some fashion for e-mail to work, so they might want to make sure they have an active Internet connection through a modem or an Ethernet connection. Occasionally, the mail server through which the e-mail is being routed becomes too busy, and e-mail might work very slowly or not at all (the equivalent here is the local post office the day before Christmas). In this event, teachers must contact their lab administrators.

As one (bad) running joke puts it: "The busiest person on the net is the Mailer Daemon. He mails everyone!" The Mailer Daemon is an automated message service that accompanies any "bounced" message. Typically, messages bounce because the e-mail address of the recipient was entered incorrectly. The message will "bounce" back to the sender's account just as traditional mail (snail mail) gets returned to the sender if the address does not exist. The message may include other information, such as when it bounced, why it bounced, and other information (contained in the header of the message, and including information about the route the message took, and so on). Figure D-1 displays an example of a message from the Mailer Daemon. In this example, the message "bounced" because it was sent to an invalid e-mail address (noone@nowhere.edu).

```
Mail Delivery Subsystem wrote:

 The original message was received at Thu, 25 Feb 1999 15:40:09 -0600
(CST)
 from xxx.xxx.niu.edu

  ----- The following addresses had permanent fatal errors -----

 <noone@nowhere.edu>

  ----- Transcript of session follows -----
 550 <noone@nowhere.edu>... Host unknown (Name server: nowhere.edu.:
host not found)

 --------------------------------------------------------------
 Reporting-MTA: dns; xxx.xxx.niu.edu
 Received-From-MTA: dns; xxx.xxxl.niu.edu
 Arrival-Date: Thu, 25 Feb 1999 15:40:09 -0600 (CST)
```

Figure D-1: "Bounced" E-mail Message Header

Messages can also bounce if a recipient's mailbox is full. That is, most e-mail accounts have a set space limit. When that limit is exceeded, no new e-mail messages can get in the box, so it bounces.

Users may also have problems sending e-mail to a mailing list or newsgroup for a few different reasons. Mailing lists and newsgroups can be set up a different ways, and some do not allow general posting. Normally, if users get a "forbidden" or "permission denied" message, this indicates that the user is not authorized to post documents to that list or newsgroup.

Receiving

Receiving e-mail can be a bit trickier than sending e-mail, or at least, more prone to problems. The most common problem users have receiving e-mail is that they forget or lose their e-mail password. Without the password, the mail server will not allow users access to their e-mail folders. Resetting this password must be done by a system administrator, so is something of a hassle, and takes some time to complete. Some recent e-mail programs (particularly Web-based programs) include a "mnemonic device feature" which asks users to think of a question or key word that relates to their password. If the user then forgets his or her password, the question or key word is supposed to jog his or her memory.[26] Again, we strongly recommend that users write down their usernames and passwords in a safe location to avoid these kinds of unpleasant situations. If students are sure they are using the correct password, check to see if the CAPS LOCK button (on the keyboard) is active; passwords are normally case sensitive. Students can also double check the e-mail setting to assure that they are trying to log into the correct account (in other words, check to make sure their usernames are entered correctly).

Assuming that the user has not forgotten the password, however, and is logging correctly into the e-mail account, some problems can still exist. First, if the e-mail account is full, then it may "lock." As we explained above, most e-mail accounts have a fixed size limit. Let's say Bob has an account that can hold 500 K (Kilobytes) of data (that's roughly enough to hold between 200 and 400 messages). Let's further assume that Bob has been away for a vacation, and his account has filled with messages (Bob is

---

[26] This "mnemonic device feature" is actually most useful for those of us who have three or more e-mail accounts, and sometimes confuse which password belongs with which account.

popular). Sometimes, accounts let you go "over limit" for a brief period, in case you need a day or two to save files locally. Well, Bob has been in Tibet for three weeks, so his grace period has long since expired, and Bob's mail account is now locked (that is, frozen by a system administrator). Bob probably will have to call the system administrator to get the problem fixed. Note that a single message can easily fill a user's inbox if it is big enough. Normal e-mail messages are very small (about one K per page of text), but since users can ATTACH almost anything to e-mail, students could receive a 15 M (one Megabyte is equivalent to 1000 K, so 15 M equals 15,000 K, or enough to fill about 11 floppy disks) picture or animation file as an attachment. Such a file would probably fill up most users' mailboxes. Unfortunately, this scenario is not at all hypothetical.

Receiving attachments raises another whole set of problems, but we'll just deal with those that might occur in a composition class. Some attachments transfer easily, and can be displayed "in-line"; that is, within the body of the email message itself. Others must be saved locally to a hard disk or floppy disk, and then opened through the appropriate program. A number of things can go wrong in this transfer process. First, the file must be "attached" correctly; that is, in the correct manner, and as a legitimate file type. (Text files can be uploaded as ASCII transfers, but graphics and executable programs must be uploaded as BINARY transfers). Second, the file has to be readable on the recipient computer. Practically speaking, if a student sends a document written in Claris Works or Microsoft Word '97, then the recipient of those documents must be able to open that kind of document. This may seem an obvious point, but students often overlook the obvious.

World Wide Web Troubleshooting

<u>File Not Found</u>

There are many potentials for errors when looking at Web pages, but the most common is when students cannot access the page they are trying to find. This situation happens with great frequency, and can be caused by three different kinds of problems.

The first kind of error happens if a user mistypes a URL. If the error is made in the first part of the URL, the error message will talk about the "DNS" entry. For example, if a student were trying to access the official White House Web site, they might type <http://www.whitehouse.orh>. The student would receive an error message that says something like "The server does not have a DNS entry. Check the server name and try again." This message simply means that the address which the student has typed does not exist, which is true, because "orh" is not a domain (the student should have typed "org" instead of "orh").

If the user mistypes the URL somewhere in the FILE PATH of the document (see Chapter 8 for more information about URLs), then the message might say something like "404: File Not Found," or some variation of that message. Sometimes, the error message might say "Forbidden," which would lead most users to believe that there is some sort of permission problem, but in fact, the "Forbidden" message can simply mean that the page as specified in the URL does not exist.

The obvious solution to this problem is to have the student carefully check the URL of the document they are trying to access, recalling that the syntax of the URL must be perfect (users cannot add spaces, change capitalization, or add punctuation to a URL, or the address will not work -- and of course, actual misspellings produce errors).

The second kind of problem happens when the user enters the URL perfectly, but the page or server itself no longer exists at that location (because the site moved or no longer exists at all). If the user receives a "DNS error" message and is sure that the spelling and syntax of the URL is perfect, then the link is truly dead and gone (because the server itself no longer exists at that location). If the error is a "file not found" variety of message, then users can attempt to "backtrack" the URL (see Chapter 8 for more information about "backtracking") and attempt to see if the page has been renamed or moved somewhere else on the same server.

The third kind of problem concerns the local ("client") computer itself. In order to access a remote Web page, the computer being used needs to have both an active Internet connection (through a modem or similar connection), AND the specific software and "language" needed to process that connection. For example, if a student were using a computer with a modem to access Internet pages, but forgot to "dial-in," the student would not be able to browse the Web, and would in fact receive a "DNS entry" error message, exactly as described in either of the cases above. This is an obvious example, but serves to illustrate the point. Users who suspect this problem to be the case should try to access different Web pages or even e-mail to see if they can connect to anything.

Note that even if the user dialed-in correctly, several things can go wrong to prevent Internet access. Most computers use a special programming "language" (usually PPP or TCP/IP) to "talk" to the Internet. If a problem develops with this "language," the computer will not be able to access the Internet, regardless of its modem. If the computer seems unable to make any sort of Internet connection, the user should call their local technical support team.

Without going into too much more detail, users confronted with these "File Not Found" kinds of problems should take the following steps:

1. Make sure the URL is typed correctly (exactly). If not, fix the spelling and try again.
2. Try to backtrack the URL and see if the page can be found in another way.
3. Make sure the computer has an active Internet connection by visiting another Web page, or checking e-mail. If not, users should contact tech support and use another machine if possible.

File Type Unknown

Occasionally, when users click on a link, they get a window that pops up telling them that the "File Type" is unknown, and prompts the user for further action (usually asking the user if they want to SAVE the file, or GET A PLUG-IN). This window is basically telling the user that the Web browser does not recognize the type of file they are trying to access. Just as word-processing programs "recognize" certain kinds of files, and can "translate" many file types into readable forms, so do Web browsers "recognize" certain file types. By default, all Web browsers recognize HTML files, JPG and GIF images, and TXT (text only) files. Web pages can contain many other kinds of files, however, such as WAVs (sounds), MOVs (movies), AVIs (another kind of movie), and even word-processing documents saved in PDF (portable document format). Browsers can handle such recognition in three ways: by using a plug-in to display the file in the Web browser itself, by opening the file in a specified application, or by saving the unrecognized file to disk.

Some Web pages use multi-media components (sounds, animations, or movies) that require special programs called plug-ins that expand the capabilities of the Web browser. When a user enters such a page, or clicks on a link that opens such a component, the Web browser may recognize the kind of file being referenced, but also recognize that the user does not have the "plug-in" required to open the file. In such a case, the Web browser itself will identify the plug-in required to display the file in question, and prompt the user to a page that allows the user to download and install the plug-in (Figure D-2).

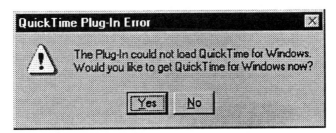

Figure D-2: Plug-in Dialogue Window

For example, let's say that we are reading a page about Stephen King's movie *Carrie*, and we notice that we can watch a small clip of the movie by clicking on a link that says "carrie.rm". When we click on the link, our Web browser opens a small window explaining that the file in question is a RealMovie type file, and that we do not have a RealPlayer installed on our computer. The window will probably offer us the option of connecting to the RealPlayer home page, where we can download and install the plug-in for free. We do so, and then watch the movie clip successfully.

If the file being accessed is not a Web multi-media application, the browser might still "recognize" the type of file (this recognition is usually related to the files recognized by the computer itself). In this case, the browser will ask the user if the file should be opened using the appropriate program or saved to disk.

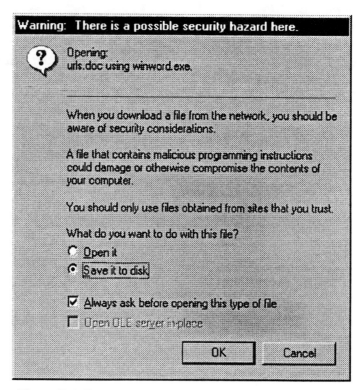

Figure D-3: Internet Download Security Dialogue Window

Figure D-3 displays such a window; note that the browser recognizes opening such files as a potential security hazard, and that users should open the file only if they are confident that the file itself contains no viruses. If the user chooses to open the file, the designated program will automatically launch and open the document in question. The user can also click the SAVE option, and the file will be saved to disk. Users should be aware that files saved to disk also pose a security hazard, so should be careful about the kinds of files they download and scan suspicious files with a virus program BEFORE opening them.

The third possibility concerns file types that the browser does not recognize at all. When a user attempts to access such a document, the Web browser might ask the user for more information about the file (such as whether the user wishes to try to find a plug-in to view the file), or simply provide the user a SAVE AS Dialogue window to download the file to a local disk. Figure D-4 displays an unknown file type window.

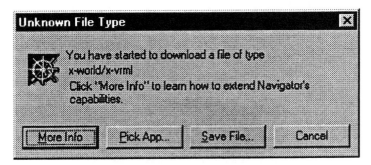

Figure D-4: Unknown File Type Dialogue Window

When confronted with this sort of window, users should just download the file, and try to open it from within the appropriate program on their computers. Again, users should be very careful about ANY files they download off the Internet, as unknown files can sometimes contain viruses or other nasty effects.

Appendix E

(A very selective list of) On-line Writing and Grammar Resources

The Writer's Workshop
Hosted by UIUC, this site proves what a premier flagship university can do with technology. This site is amazingly good, providing all sorts of on-line writing help. Go here. Now. Really.
<http://www.english.uiuc.edu/cws/wworkshop/writer.html>

The University of Victoria's Hypertext Writer's Guide
One of the best available sets of hyperlinked references on all aspects of writing.
<http://webserver.maclab.comp.uvic.ca/writersguide/welcome.html>

Reference Materials on the Writing Center at Colorado State University
This site is a huge framed collection of writing resources, organized and mostly published out of Colorado State U. I recommend this site very highly. Though browsing through the frames can get old quickly, the consequent organization is worth the hassle.
<http://www.colostate.edu/Depts/WritingCenter/reference.htm>

Guide to Grammar and Writing
Though as the name implies, this site is more appropriately a grammar site, this site does provide a number of more general writing resources. I really like this site; it's easily the best grammar guide around, and the webmaster includes a variety of very cool things for the writer.
<http://webster.commnet.edu/HP/pages/darling/grammar.htm>

Elements of Style
The Strunk classic. Still one of the better writing guides around, though not as complete as some of the other sites listed above.
<http://www.cc.columbia.edu/acis/bartleby/strunk/>

Purdue On-line Writing Lab
Purdue's famous OWL, useful for general writing concerns. This site contains an impressive number of on-line "hand-outs."
<http://owl.english.purdue.edu/writers/by-topic.html>

University of Wisconsin On-line Writing Center
Like Purdue, the University of Wisconsin at Madison offers a variety of writing resources, including information about Writing Across the Curriculum.
<http://www.wisc.edu/writetest/Handbook/>

On-Line English Grammar
This site, hosted by edunet, is another very good site devoted to English grammar.
<http://www.edunet.com/english/grammar/index.html>

Traditional English Grammar
This site really tests your knowledge of grammar with an excellent set of interactive quizzes. The site also has a very helpful FAQ file.
<http://www.niu.edu/english/deh/207t.html>

The Hypertext Book for English 126 Modern English Grammar
This set of pages by Daniel Kies is a truly impressive testament to the possibilities of using the Web for teaching. Users can also link to his other excellent Web sites for his composition courses.
<http://www.cod.edu/dept/kiesdan/engl_126/book126.htm>

The Forest of Rhetoric (silva rhetoricae)
"This online rhetoric, provided by Dr. Gideon Burton of Brigham Young University, is a guide to the terms of classical and renaissance rhetoric. . . .The site is intended to help beginners, as well as experts, make sense of rhetoric." (Text taken from page description).
<http://humanities.byu.edu/rhetoric/silva.htm>

Grammar Girl's Guide to the English Language
A fun and cute approach to grammar instruction.
<http://www.geocities.com/Athens/Parthenon/1489/index.html>

Appendix F

Select Bibliography

Abilock, Debbie. "Choose the Best Search Engine for Your Information Needs." The Nueva School, 19 January 1999. <http://www.nueva.pvt.k12.ca.us/~debbie/library/research/adviceengine.html> February 1999.

Amato, Vito, J. Michael Blocher, and Jon Stroslee. *An Interactive Guide to the Internet.* Indianapolis: Que Education and Training, 1996.

Anderson, Daniel. "From Browsers to Builders: Student Composition on the World Wide Web," *CWRL, The Electronic Journal for Computer Writing, Rhetoric and Literature.* Computer Writing and Research Lab, University of Texas at Austin, 4 August 1995. <http://www.cwrl.utexas.edu/~daniel/browserstobuilders/> February 1999.

---. "Not Maimed but Malted: Nodes, Text and Graphics in Freshmen Compositions." *CWRL, The Electronic Journal for Computer Writing, Rhetoric and Literature.* Computer Writing and Research Lab, University of Texas at Austin, 4 August 1995. <http://www.cwrl.utexas.edu/~cwrl/v1n1/article1/notmaimedbutmalted.html> January 1999.

Barker, Florence G. "Integrating Computer Usage in the Classroom Curriculum Through Teacher Training." *Practicum Report*, Nova Southeastern Univ. June 1994. ED 372 751.

Barker, Thomas T. and Fred O. Kemp. "Network Theory: A Postmodern Pedagogy for the Writing Classroom." *Computers and Community: Teaching Composition in the Twenty-First Century.* Ed. Carolyn Handa. Portsmouth, NH: Boynton/Cook, 1990. 1-27.

Barlow, Linda. "The Spider's Apprentice: Tips on Searching the Web." Monash Information Services, 10 November 1998. <http://www.monash.com/spidap.html> February 1999.

Bebak, Arthur and Bud E. Smith. *Creating Web Pages for Dummies.* 3rd Ed. IDG Books Worldwide, 1998.

Beck, Susan E. "The Good, The Bad and The Ugly, or, Why It's a Good Idea to Evaluate Web Sources." New Mexico State University Library, 14 October 1998. <http://lib.nmsu.edu/staff/susabeck/eval.html> February 1999.

Bump, Jerome. "Radical Changes in Class Discussion Using Networked Computers." *Computers and the Humanities.* 24 (1990): 49-65.

Burns, Joe. "The Goodies HTML Banner Primers." HTML Goodies.com, 1998. <http://www.htmlgoodies.com/primers/basics.html> February 1999.

Carey, Doris M. "Teacher Roles and Technology Integration: Moving from Teacher as Director to Teacher as Facilitator." *Computers in the Schools.* 9.2/3 (1993): 105-117.

Carvin, Andy. "Homeroom," *The EdWeb Home Room @ SunSITE USA.* UNC Metalab, 1998. <http://metalab.unc.edu/edweb/resource.cntnts.html> February 1999.

Castro, Elizabeth. *HTML 4 for the World Wide Web: Visual QuickStart Guide.* Nancy Davis, ed. Peachpit Press, 1998.

Chapman, Ron, et al. *Educator's Internet Yellow Pages.* Upper Saddle River: Prentice Hall Computer Books, 1996.

Ciolek, T.Matthew and Irena M. Goltz. "Information Quality WWW Virtual Library: The Internet Guide to Construction of Quality Online Resources." WWW.CIOLEK.COM: Asia Pacific Research Online, 26 January 1999. <http://www.ciolek.com/WWWVL-InfoQuality.html> February 1999.

Cohen, Laura and Trudi Jacobson. "Evaluating Internet Resources." University at Albany Libraries, April 1996. <http://www.albany.edu/library/internet/evaluate.html> February 1999.

Cooper, Marilyn, and Cynthia L. Selfe. "Computer Conferences and Learning: Authority, Resistance, and Internally Persuasive Discourse." *College English.* (52): 1990. 847-869.

Cosgrave, Tony, Michael Engle and Joan Ormondroyd. "How to Critically Analyze Information Sources." Reference Services Division, Olin*Kroch*Uris Libraries, Cornell University Library, 20 October 1996. <http://www.library.cornell.edu/okuref/research/skill26.htm> February 1999.

December, John. *CMC Information Sources.* December Communications, Inc., 23 December 1997. <http://www.december.com/cmc/info/> February 1999.

DeVoss, Danielle, ed. "Computers and Composition Comprehensive Bibliography," *Computers and Composition: An International Journal for Teachers of Writing.* Michigan Technological University Humanities Department, 1998. <http://www.hu.mtu.edu/~candc/bib/index.htm> February 1999.

Eldred, Janet M. "Computers and Pedagogy: Pedagogy in the Computer-Networked Classroom." *Computers and Composition.* 8.2 (April 1991): 47-61.

Fey, Marion Harris, and Michael J. Sisson. "Approaching the Information Superhighway: Internet Collaboration Among Future Writing Teachers." *Computers and Composition*. 13.1 (1996): 37-47.

Giagnocavo, Gregory, ed. *Educator's Internet Companion: Classroom Connect's Complete Guide to Educational Resources on the Internet.* Upper Saddle River: Prentice Hall Computer Books, 1996.

Glavac, Marjan M. *The Busy Educator's Guide To The World Wide Web.* NIMA Systems, 1998.

Grassian, Esther. "Thinking Critically about World Wide Web Resources." UCLA College Library, October 1998. <http://www.library.ucla.edu/libraries/college/instruct/web/critical.htm> February 1999.

Handa, Carolyn. *Computers and Community:Teaching Composition in the Twenty-First Century.* Portsmouth, NJ: Boynton/Cook, 1990.

Harris, Robert. "Evaluating Internet Research Sources." Southern California College, 17 November 1997. <http://www.sccu.edu/faculty/R_Harris/evalu8it.htm> December 1998.

Hawisher, Gail E. "Cross-Disciplinary Perspectives: Computer-Mediated Communication (CMC), Electronic Writing Classes, and Research." *SIGCUE Outlook* 21.3 (1992): 45-52.

---. and Charles Moran. "Electronic Mail and the Writing Instructor." *College English* 55.6 (1993): 627-643.

---. and Cynthia L. Selfe, eds. *Evolving Perspective on Computers and Composition Studies: Questions for the 1990s.* Urbana, IL: NCTE, 1991.

Hinchliffe, Lisa Janicke. "Resource Selection and Information Evaluation." The Graduate School of Library and Information Science at the University of Illinois at Urbana-Champaign, 29 May 1997. <http://alexia.lis.uiuc.edu/~janicke/Evaluate.html> February 1999.

Holeton, Richard. *Composing Cyberspace: Identity, Community, and Knowledge in the Electronic Age.* New York: McGraw Hill, 1998.

"HTML Tag Reference," *DevEdge Online Documentation.* Netscape Communications, 1998. <http://developer.netscape.com/docs/manuals/htmlguid/index.htm> February 1999.

Joyce, Michael. "New Teaching: Toward a Pedagogy for a New Cosmology." *Computers and Composition.* 9.2 (1992): 7-16.

Keenan, Claudine. "An Educator's Guide to the Internet." Pennsylvania State University, Center for Academic Computing, 3 November 1996. <http://cac.psu.edu/~cgk4/design.html> February 1999.

Kemp, Fred. "Writing Dialogically: Bold Lessons from Electronic Text." *Reconceiving Writing, ReThinking Writing Instruction.* Ed. Joseph Petraglia-Bahri and Lawrence Erlbaum, 1995.

Klem, Elizabeth and Charles Moran. "Teachers in a Strange LANd: Learning to Teach in a Networked Writing Classroom." *Computers and Composition* 9.3 (1992): 5-22.

Madden, Ed. "Women, Gods, and Monsters: Using Hypertexts in the Literature Classroom," *CWRL, The Electronic Journal for Computer Writing, Rhetoric and Literature.* Computer Writing and Research Lab, University of Texas at Austin, Spring 1995. <http://www.cwrl.utexas.edu/~cwrl/v1n2/article3/madden.html> February 1999.

McFedries, Paul. *The Complete Idiot's Guide to Creating an Html 4 Web Page.* 3rd Ed. Book and Cdrom. Que Education & Training, 1997.

McKim, Geoffrey W. *Internet Research Companion.* Indianapolis: Que Education & Training, 1996.

McManus, Thomas Fox. "Delivering Instruction on the World Wide Web." University of Texas at Austin, 19 January 1996. <http://ccwf.cc.utexas.edu/~mcmanus/wbi.html> February 1999.

"NCSA—A Beginner's Guide to HTML Home Page." National Center for Supercomputing Applications, 1998. <http://www.ncsa.uiuc.edu/General/Internet/WWW/HTMLPrimer.html> February 1999.

Richmond, Betsy. "Ten C's for Evaluating Internet Resources." University of Wisconsin-Eau Claire, McIntyre Library, 20 November 1996. <http://www.uwec.edu/Admin/Library/10cs.html> February 1999.

Roerden, Laura Parker. "Net Lessons: Web-Based Projects for Your Classroom." Ed. Sheryl Avruch. O'Reilly & Associates, 1997.

Selfe, Richard. "What Are They Talking About? Computer Terms That English Teachers May Need to Know." *Re-Imagining Computers and Composition: Teaching and Research in the Virtual Age.* Ed. Gail E. Hawisher and Paul LeBlanc. Portsmouth, NH: Boynton/Cook, 1992. 207-218.

Stegall, Nancy L. "Using Cybersources." DeVry Institute of Technology, Online Writing Support Center, 31 August 1998. <http://www.devry-phx.edu/lrnresrc/dowsc/integrty.htm> February 1999.

Tillman, Hope N. "Evaluating Quality on the Net." TIAC: The Internet Access Company, Inc., 2 January 1999. <http://www.tiac.net/users/hope/findqual.html> February 1999.

Yagelski, Robert P. and Sarah Powley. "Virtual Connections and Real Boundaries: Teaching Writing and Preparing Writing Teachers on the Internet." *Computers and Composition.* 13.1 (1996): 25-36.

Screen-shot permissions

All Netscape Screenshots used with permission of Netscape Communications Corporation. Copyright 1999 Netscape Communications Corporation. All rights reserved.
All Microsoft Screen shots reprinted by permission from Microsoft Corporation.
Figure 9-4 reprinted by permission from O'Reilly Corporation.
Figure 5-4 reprinted by permission from University of Washington.
Figure 9-5 reprinted by permission from Jeanne McWhorter.
Figure B-9 NIU logo reprinted by permission from Northern Illinois University.

NOTES

NOTES

NOTES

NOTES

NOTES

NOTES

NOTES

NOTES

NOTES

NOTES

NOTES